VEGAN
COOKING

pi

Publications International, Ltd.

Pictured on the front cover: Persimmon and Chickpea Salad *(page 110)*.

Pictured on the back cover *(clockwise from top left):* Avocado Toast *(page 17),* Pineapple Upside Down Cake *(page 219),* Green Beans with Garlic-Cilantro Sauce *(page 96)* and Chickpea Tikka Masala *(page 210).*

Photographs and art on front cover and pages 5, 9, 10, 11, 14 (right), 15 (bottom), 65, 67, 105 and 107 copyright © Shutterstock.com.

ISBN: 978-1-64030-887-9

Manufactured in China.

8 7 6 5 4 3 2 1

Let's get social!

 @Publications_International

 @PublicationsInternational

www.pilcookbooks.com

CONTENTS

INTRODUCTION 4

BREAKFAST, SMOOTHIES & JUICES 16

SNACKS, SMALL BITES & BREADS 38

SALADS & VEGETABLES 72

SOUPS, STEWS & CHILIES 114

SANDWICHES, TACOS & WRAPS 138

CURRIES, NOODLES & STIR-FRIES 158

BOWLS 192

DESSERTS 218

INDEX 250

INTRODUCTION

THE FIRST VEGAN

The word "vegan" was coined by Donald Watson, a British woodworker. Watson became a vegetarian at the age of 12 after seeing a pig slaughtered on his uncle's farm in Yorkshire, England. He and his wife Dorothy founded the Vegan Society in 1944. Looking for a name for a vegetarian diet that also excluded other animal products, he put together letters from the beginning and end of the word "vegetarian" to spell "vegan," a word now found in most dictionaries.

THE PLEASURES OF VEGAN COOKING

Vegan, at least as defined for this book, means consuming no animal products—no meat, poultry, fish, dairy, eggs or honey. There are many different kinds of vegans and even more reasons for becoming one, from ethics to weight control. Of course there are also plenty of compelling health and environmental reasons for giving up animal products, but one of the unsung joys of cooking vegan dishes is the incredible flavor you'll discover—the plant kingdom offers so much variety in terms of color, taste and texture. When a meal isn't centered around meat, it's easier to appreciate the sweet tenderness of a roasted beet or the crunch of just-picked sugar snap peas. The recipes in this book were chosen to help make vegan cooking and eating not just healthy, but truly delicious. Becoming vegan should be about wonderful new dishes to discover, not about food you have to give up.

ALL KINDS OF VEGANS FOR ALL KINDS OF REASONS

This book is not just for dedicated vegans but also for those who want to try out a new way to cook and eat. The recipes use no animal products—no meat, fish, dairy, eggs, honey or gelatin. Health is the most common reason for eating a plant-based diet. A diet filled with veggies, fruits, grains and nuts tends to be lower in fat and higher in fiber and antioxidants. Concern for animals is also a big part of the motivation. Many feel that it is morally indefensible to kill animals for food. For others, the very idea of meat becomes repulsive once they know about factory farms, mad-cow disease, E. coli contamination and the like.

A recent study estimates that 3.2 percent of the adults in the U.S. (about 7.3 million people) follow a vegetarian-based diet. Estimates put the number of vegans in that pool at about 1 million (and growing fast!). Millions more want the benefits of a vegan diet but aren't ready to commit to it 100 percent. Being vegan, at least some of the time, is being embraced by more and more people from rock stars to ex-presidents.

BECOMING VEGAN

It doesn't require a degree in nutrition, joining a club or giving up dinner with friends. Being on a vegan diet simply means that you don't eat anything that comes from an animal. Of course there are animal products other than food that are part of our lives—leather shoes, tallow in soap and lanolin in lip balm, for example. Those who espouse a totally vegan lifestyle often choose to avoid animal products in every part of their lives. This book only addresses the dietary part of the equation.

BUT WHAT WILL I EAT?

Gone are the days when a vegan had to visit a strange smelling, brightly lit health food store to buy provisions. Now any decent size market stocks soymilk, quinoa, veggie burgers and even seitan. Don't think about replacing meat; instead, consider all the wonderful vegetables, grains, fruits and nuts you will enjoy. A quick look through the recipes in this book will convince you that dishes like Mushroom Gratin (page 174) or Chickpea Tikka Masala (page 210) are every bit as satisfying (and considerably better for you!) than another dinner of ground beef or chicken nuggets.

PLANNING VEGAN MEALS

For some time now, American meals have consisted of a main course—meat—accompanied by sides. The newly minted vegan may, at first, simply replace the center-of-the-plate meat with a veggie lasagna or tofu dog. A meal certainly doesn't have to be structured that way. It doesn't even have to be served on one big plate! In fact, most cuisines around the world are considerably less meat-centric. In Chinese and Japanese cooking, meat is more often a condiment or flavoring agent than the star of the show. The Middle East has its small plates called mezes and Spain specializes in tapas. Vegan meals work well as a series of individual dishes that complement each other without a single item stealing the show. Soup and salad can be a filling and delightful dinner. A colorful stir-fry could be the centerpiece for an elegant dinner party. The possibilities are endless.

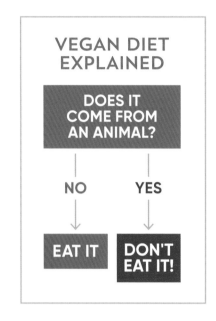

VEGAN DIET EXPLAINED

DOES IT COME FROM AN ANIMAL?

NO   YES

EAT IT   **DON'T EAT IT!**

Honey seems innocent enough but since it is made by bees it is considered an animal product and therefore not vegan. It is easy to replace—just use maple syrup or agave nectar instead.

VEGAN FAQS

1 **Isn't it hard to become vegan?**
It can be if you try to change everything overnight. Instead approach it gradually and positively. Every day that you don't eat animal products is a step in the right direction for your health, animal welfare and the environment. You can start by going vegetarian first, or try going vegan for a few days a week.

2 **Is a vegan diet expensive?**
It certainly doesn't have to be. Meat is an expensive part of the typical American diet. Meat and dairy substitutes can be pricey, but seasonal produce, beans, rice and pasta are certainly affordable.

3 **Must I take vitamin supplements?**
Not necessarily. See page 8 for nutritional information. According to the American Dietetic Association, "...appropriately planned vegetarian diets, including total vegetarian or vegan diets, are healthful, nutritionally adequate, and may provide health benefits in the prevention and treatment of certain diseases."

4 **Do I have to give up chocolate?**
Chocolate comes from a plant—the cocoa bean—so it starts out vegan. However, a lot of chocolate products have milk solids or milk fat added. The good news is that high-quality dark chocolate usually contains nothing more than cocoa, cocoa butter and sugar, so feel free to indulge.

5 **What do I tell friends who invite me for dinner?**
Explain that you don't eat animal products. Most cooks want to know about dietary preferences and are used to making allowances for vegetarians and those with food allergies. Just don't expect everything on the menu to be vegan.

6 **What about eating out?**
More and more restaurants offer vegetarian and even vegan menu options. Online sources can help you find those in your area. For fast food options, your best bets are Asian or Mexican eateries that will prepare a stir-fry or burrito to order.

7 **But I love to bake. How can I do that without eggs or milk?**
Don't despair or throw away your old cookbooks. Most recipes can easily be converted. See pages 10–11 for information on dairy and egg substitutes.

8 **What about bread? Is yeast vegan?**
Yeast is a one-celled fungus and just as vegan as a mushroom. In fact, yeast cells are in the air all around us, which is how naturally leavened breads are made. However, many packaged breads on supermarket shelves do contain milk products or eggs. Stick with European-style baguettes or ciabatta and read labels carefully.

THE HEALTHY VEGAN DIET

The key to any healthy diet is variety. A vegan diet consisting of pasta and potato chips would certainly not provide the vitamins, minerals and other nutrients human bodies need. A diet of fast food burgers, fried chicken and soda would be even worse! For vegans, variety means eating plenty of fruits, vegetables, leafy greens, whole grains, nuts, seeds and legumes.

MORE OF THE GOOD STUFF

Eliminating animal products from your diet gets rid of most sources of cholesterol and saturated fats. Better yet, without meat you'll probably eat more high-fiber grains, fruits and vegetables. Every food pyramid and healthy-eating expert agrees that eating a variety of colorful produce is good for you. Phytonutrients give food a rainbow of colors, and ongoing research seems to indicate they can be helpful in preventing disease and boosting immune systems. Carotinoids provide yellow and orange colors and are powerful antioxidants. Think carrots and squash. Tomatoes and watermelon are red because they contain lycopene, which may fight cancer. Resveratrol from purple grapes and wine is another antioxidant. There's no need to get a degree in nutrition—just enjoy a colorful variety of foods every day.

THE PROTEIN PROBLEM THAT ISN'T

If you've been a vegan for a while, you've probably been asked, "But what do you do about protein?" Our meat-centric society thinks of beef, pork, chicken and milk as the only good sources of protein. Plant foods actually provide plenty of protein—check the nutritional listings for tofu, lentils or quinoa if you need reassurance. Decades ago nutritionists believed that since meat contained all the essential amino acids (the ones our body can't produce on its own), vegetarians needed to eat a combination of foods at each meal that provided this same assortment. It was complicated and soon found to be totally unnecessary—your metabolism takes care of combining for you. In fact, most Americans eat too much protein, which can be unhealthy!

TIPS TO KEEP VEGAN DIETS INTERESTING

1 Serve three or four small plates instead of one main course with sides.

2 Go ethnic. Explore Asian noodle dishes like Soba Stir-Fry (page 160) or try Mexican bean dishes like Black Bean Soup (page 115).

3 Give potatoes and pasta a rest. Try adding couscous, quinoa or bulgur wheat instead.

4 Experiment with meat replacements. In addition to tofu, try tempeh, seitan or texturized soy protein (pages 12–13).

5 Cook with the seasons. Take advantage of farmers' markets and enjoy more fresh produce.

6 Go nuts! Spread nut butters on your toast. Add toasted almonds or walnuts to your cereal, salad, casserole or stir-fry.

KNOW YOUR NUTRIENTS

Here's a list of good sources of nutrients sometimes lacking in a vegan diet.

PROTEIN
- legumes
- lentils
- soy products
- whole grains

CALCIUM
- almonds
- broccoli
- fortified orange juice
- kale
- tahini
- tofu

VITAMIN B$_{12}$
- enriched dairy-free milks
- enriched nutritional yeast
- fortified cereals

OMEGA-3 FATTY ACIDS
- flaxseed
- olive oil
- tofu
- walnuts

IRON*
- brussels sprouts
- blackstrap molasses
- edamame
- kidney beans
- lentils
- turmeric

*To enhance iron absorption, combine foods with those rich in Vitamin C.

IMPORTANT NUTRIENTS FOR VEGANS

CALCIUM AND VITAMIN D
Do we need to drink milk to get enough calcium as the dairy industry tries to convince us? Fortunately there are many plant sources for calcium; many of them provide magnesium and potassium as well, which are also vital for bone health. Collard greens, tahini, broccoli and fortified dairy-free milk are just a few plant sources of calcium. Vitamin D is also necessary for strong bones. Exposure to sunlight is one way to get it. The only plant source is mushrooms, but Vitamin D is also often added to fortified dairy-free milks, cereals and orange juice.

VITAMIN B$_{12}$
Vitamin B$_{12}$ is found only in animal foods. Fortunately there are many vegan foods that are fortified with this important vitamin responsible for cell division and blood formation. Check labels, but dairy-free milks, cereals, meat substitutes and nutritional yeast are often fortified. You can also take a supplement. The good news is that we require only a small amount of B$_{12}$ and can store and recycle it. However, absorption rates of B$_{12}$ from food or supplements can vary from 50 percent to 0.5 percent. Consult a doctor or nutritionist if you are concerned.

OMEGA-3 FATTY ACIDS
There are three different types of omega-3 fatty acids. ALA is found in plant sources like flaxseed, tofu and walnuts. The other two types are EPA and DHA, which come from oily fish. DHA is the type that is most researched and seems to have the most health benefits. Our bodies can convert ALA into the beneficial DHA but it requires more metabolic work, so you need to consume more ALA if you are vegan to achieve the same level of DHA as a fish eater. There are vegan DHA supplements available made from algae.

IRON
There are many plant sources of iron, including dried fruits, nuts, green leafy vegetables, beans, whole grains and blackstrap molasses. Using cast iron pots and pans can also contribute iron to the food cooked in them.

THE VEGAN PANTRY

All cooking depends on the quality of ingredients—even more so if it's vegan. The sometimes subtle flavors of fresh produce need to be coaxed and complemented, not overwhelmed. Use cheap oil or a dusty jar of dried basil and it will be easy to tell. The flavor of meat can mask a multitude of sins!

ADVANCED LABEL READING

Skip over the advertising claims on package labels like "natural," "cruelty-free" and "earth friendly." These are generally meaningless. The real information is in the ingredient list in very small type. It's easy to spot meat, eggs and dairy, but multisyllabic names hidden in a lengthy list can make recognizing animal ingredients a lot trickier. Generally the longer the list, the more processed the food item, and the more likely it is to contain animal products.

Often dairy products in some form are added to commercial baked goods to improve shelf life and texture. They can be listed as casein, whey or lactose. You can always query the manufacturer or check an online list of suspect ingredients.

PANTRY ITEMS TO KEEP ON HAND:

- Agave nectar
- **Beans:** a variety of canned and/or dried
- **Bulgur wheat**
- **Chickpeas**
- **Dairy-free milk and margarine (vegan buttery spread)**
- **Ground flaxseed**
- **Lentils**
- **Mushrooms:** fresh and dried
- **Noodles and pasta**
- **Nutritional yeast**
- **Nuts:** almonds, cashews, walnuts
- **Oils:** extra virgin olive oil, vegetable oil
- **Rice:** long grain, brown, basmati, jasmine
- **Soy foods:** edamame, miso paste, soy sauce, tempeh, texturized soy protein, tofu
- **Tomatoes:** canned whole and diced

COOKING MINUS THE MILK

Giving up milk products is often the biggest challenge for vegans. It's easy to forget that dairy is so integral to many favorites, from the cheese on pizza to the butter in cookies. Not to mention that casein and whey, both dairy products, show up in margarine, soy cheeses and other vegetarian products. Fortunately, U.S. food manufacturers are now required to list the simple word "milk" as part of the ingredient list or in boldface type at the end of the list, even if the actual dairy ingredient goes by an obscure chemical name. The really good news is that there are more and better dairy replacement products available all the time.

DAIRY-FREE MILK

Once soymilk was your only choice. Now you can try rice milk, almond milk, coconut milk, oat milk, even hemp milk. These tasty dairy replacements can do pretty much everything milk can do. While dairy-free milks can be substituted for each other, the different flavors and textures may influence how you use them. Rice milk is slightly sweet, so it works well in dessert recipes but is not as appropriate in savory dishes. Soymilk is a good substitute in baking since it is similar to cow's milk in protein content and texture. Almond milk is rich and nutty but has a flavor profile that can clash with savory dishes.

When choosing a dairy-free milk, check the nutritional label. Most are fortified with calcium and vitamin B_{12} to bring them nutritionally closer to cow's milk. You may also want to check protein and sugar content, which vary.

DAIRY-FREE MARGARINE

Warning: Most regular margarines contain small amounts of milk products, even those labeled nondairy. Look for the word "vegan," "dairy-free" or the Kosher designation "pareve" or "parv," which means no dairy products at all. Dairy-free margarine comes in two forms: in sticks like butter and in tubs. The stick form can be used one-to-one to replace butter in baking recipes. Tub margarine often contains more water or air, so it will not measure the same as stick margarine or butter.

NONDAIRY IS NOT ALWAYS DAIRY-FREE

Many products labeled nondairy contain whey, casein or other milk-derived ingredients. According to the FDA, nondairy products can contain 0.5 percent or less of milk products by weight. Nondairy creamers and nondairy whipped toppings usually contain dairy in some form.

WHAT IS NUTRITIONAL YEAST?

Nutritional yeast is a favorite with vegetarians, especially vegans, since it has a taste similar to Parmesan cheese and can be a source of vitamin B_{12}. It is a deactivated yeast that comes in powder or flake form and can be sprinkled directly on food or used in recipes. Read labels carefully though, since only a few brands are fortified with B_{12}; look for the tongue twister cyanocobalamin (the chemical name for B_{12}).

DAIRY-FREE SOUR CREAM AND YOGURT

A little tangy sour cream or yogurt goes a long way to make dips and smoothies more satisfying, and a dollop on spicy stews can help cool the fire. A few years ago, vegan options were quite limited, but as the vegan diet has become more mainstream, more products have become available. Many dairy-free yogurts are also cultured or fortified to provide helpful probiotics.

BUT WHAT ABOUT CHEESE?!

Let's admit that cheese is one of the toughest things to replace. Sure, there are dairy-free cheeses, but many of them don't taste like the real thing and quite a few soy cheeses have casein added to help them melt better, so check the labels. There are better choices all the time, so experiment with different brands to find one you like best.

For bland cheeses like ricotta or cottage cheese, crumbled tofu is often a good stand-in. You'll also find recipes online for making your own spreadable vegan cheese from cashews or macadamia nuts, and nutritional yeast adds a savory tang to many recipes and can be sprinkled on popcorn or pasta like Parmesan cheese.

BAKING WITHOUT BUTTER OR EGGS

For most recipes the easiest replacement for butter is vegan margarine. Unrefined coconut oil, which is solid at room temperature like butter, is another option where the slight coconut flavor works. For pie crusts, choose a vegan or non-hydrogenated vegetable shortening. The easiest and most consistent replacement for eggs in baked goods is a mixture of boiling water and ground flaxseed—when it cools it thickens to a consistency like egg whites. For each egg you're replacing, combine 3 tablespoons boiling water and 1 tablespoon ground flaxseed in a small bowl and let stand until cool. In most baked goods requiring no more than three eggs, silken tofu is also an acceptable replacement. (Use ¼ cup to replace each egg.) One mashed banana or ¼ cup of applesauce can often fill in for one egg in quick breads or muffins that are sweet or fruity.

PRESSING TOFU

Drain tofu and cut it in half crosswise. Place it between layers of paper towels or folded clean kitchen towels on a cutting board. Place something flat like a baking dish or another cutting board on it and place cans or other large heavy objects on top. Let it stand for 20 to 30 minutes. Pat dry.

CRISPY BAKED TOFU

1 package (14 to 16 ounces) firm tofu

⅓ cup cornstarch

½ teaspoon salt

Drain tofu, press it and cut it into 24 (1-inch) cubes. Toss it with cornstarch and salt in large bowl. Spread on baking sheet sprayed with nonstick cooking spray. Spray tops of cubes with cooking spray. Bake at 400°F for 20 minutes or until crispy, turning once.

TOFU AND FRIENDS

Sometimes tofu, seitan and tempeh are referred to as meat substitutes. It's true that these ingredients can be made into products that resemble meat with a satisfying chew and somewhat meaty flavor. However, many vegans enjoy them because they are delicious and nutritious in and of themselves. While they are relatively recent additions to American kitchens, they have been a huge part of Asian cuisines for centuries.

TOFU

You probably know that tofu is made from soybeans, but you may be unaware that the process that produces it is very similar to making cheese. A salt- or acid-based coagulant is added to soymilk to form curds and whey. Once the curds are drained and pressed, you have a block of tofu.

Using Tofu: Tofu comes in many forms, as a visit to any Asian market will illustrate, but there are two main types. Regular or brick tofu (sometimes called Chinese tofu) is sold in the refrigerated section of the supermarket in the produce section or near the dairy case and comes sealed in a plastic tub filled with water. There is usually a choice of soft, medium, firm or extra firm. Once opened, regular tofu will keep in the refrigerator up to four days. The water should be drained and replaced daily. Silken tofu, sometimes called Japanese tofu, usually comes in an aseptic box, which does not require refrigeration. While it also comes in soft, medium or firm, the texture of silken tofu is almost custard-like compared to regular. Look for extra firm silken tofu to use in stir-fries.

TEMPEH

Tempeh (pronounced "TEM-pay") is a very nutritious fermented soy food that originated in Indonesia hundreds of years ago. Although it won't win prizes for good looks—it looks like a messy cake of beans and nuts squashed together—tempeh has a nutty, yeasty flavor and chewy texture that is easy to love. You'll find cakes of tempeh, vacuum-packed and refrigerated, in natural food stores and some supermarkets. Soybean tempeh is the classic version, but tempeh can also be made of rice and other grains, or be a mixture of soy and grain.

Using Tempeh: It's best to cook tempeh before eating it, although this is for taste reasons rather than food safety ones. Cooking improves both flavor and texture.

Like tofu, tempeh has an ability to readily absorb flavors and cooking enhances this. Its firm texture makes it a great choice to replace ground beef, cook on the grill or use in a sandwich.

SEITAN

Seiten (pronounced "SAY-tan") is sometimes called wheat-meat, gluten-meat or mock duck. It is made by washing away the starch component from wheat until only the wheat protein—gluten—is left. If you've ever eaten mock duck or mock chicken in a Chinese restaurant, you've tried seitan. It is also the base for some commercial vegetarian deli "meats."

Using Seitan: You'll find seitan in the refrigerated section of natural food stores and large supermakets near the produce section or the dairy case in a tub or a vacuum pack. It may also be found in the freezer section. Varieties are plain, flavored, Asian-style with soy and ginger, or seasoned to taste like chicken or other meat. Seitan is incredibly versatile. It can be stir-fried, baked, broiled or grilled.

TEXTURED SOY PROTEIN (TVP)

Textured soy protein is defatted soy flour and a by-product of extracting the oil from soybeans. It comes in granules, flakes, chunks and nuggets. It has a protein content and texture similar to ground beef when reconstituted.

Using TVP: To use textured soy protein it must be soaked briefly in a hot liquid. (See the recipe for Sloppy Joes on page 154.) Use granulated TVP as a substitute for ground meat in tacos, chili or pasta sauce, or form it into veggie burgers or meatballs. Larger chunks can stand in for meat in casseroles, stews or chilies.

TEMPEH BACON

- 2 tablespoons liquid aminos or soy sauce
- 1 tablespoon apple cider vinegar
- 1 tablespoon maple syrup
- 1 teaspoon liquid smoke
- 1 package (8 ounces) unflavored tempeh, cut into ¼-inch slices
- 1 tablespoon olive oil
- 1 teaspoon paprika

1. Combine all ingredients in large resealable food storage bag. Seal bag, pressing out air; turn to coat. Marinate in refrigerator at least 2 hours or overnight.

2. Preheat oven to 350°F. Line baking sheet with parchment paper. Arrange tempeh on prepared baking sheet.

3. Bake 15 minutes. Flip and bake 15 minutes or until tempeh is dry and edges are crispy.

AQUAFABA MERINGUES

- ½ cup aquafaba (liquid from can of chickpeas)
- ½ teaspoon vanilla
- ¼ teaspoon salt
- ¼ teaspoon cream of tartar
- ¾ cup sugar
- 3 tablespoons cocoa powder

1. Preheat oven to 200°F. Line 2 baking sheets with parchment paper. Whip aquafaba, vanilla, salt and cream of tartar in bowl of stand mixer with whip attachment on high speed about 5 minutes or until soft peaks form. Gradually add sugar 1 tablespoon at a time; beat 5 to 10 minutes or until thick and glossy and stiff peaks form. Add cocoa; beat until well blended.

2. Place in large food storage bag; cut off small corner. Pipe 1-inch circles on prepared baking sheets. Bake 1 hour until meringues are dry and set. Carefully peel from parchment.

VERY VEGAN, VERY DELICIOUS

Most people who say they can't imagine what vegans eat lack imagination themselves! The plant kingdom offers choices of color, texture and taste that go way beyond the dull beige world of meat. Here are some ideas for adding flavor and fun to your vegan diet.

AGAR AGAR

This amazing ingredient can do anything gelatin can do better and without animal products. It's made from seaweed and has been used in Asian cuisines for centuries. Agar agar has little taste of its own, so it works in sweet or savory dishes. It will set at room temperature and stay set when warm. In addition, it retains some of the nutrients of seaweed.

AGAVE NECTAR

This natural sweetener is made from a cactus-like plant. Agave nectar has a delicate flavor and syrupy consistency, which make it an excellent substitute for honey or white sugar.

COCONUT MILK

Coconut milk makes a rich, creamy vegan substitute for milk products in cooking. Look for unsweetened coconut milk in cans in the Asian section of the supermarket. (Coconut water is a much thinner liquid and is sold for drinking, not cooking.)

FLAXSEED

Versatile flaxseed is rich in alpha linolenic acid, the plant version of omega-3 fatty acids. Add ground flaxseed to hot or cold cereal, a smoothie or soy yogurt. Add it to baked goods or use it as an egg replacer (see page 11).

Aquafaba Meringues

KALE

Finally kale has become trendy and is being appreciated for more than just its excellent nutritional profile. Add kale to any pasta, potato, grain or bean dish for color and flavor. Enjoy the frilly green leaves in a salad, simmered or sautéed.

MISO

This fermented soy-based seasoning paste has a buttery texture and a tangy, salty taste. In addition to soup, miso is also used for dressings, marinades and sauces.

NUTRITIONAL YEAST

It won't make bread rise or expand in your tummy because it's an inactive version of yeast, but this magical ingredient is a favorite with many vegans. Nutritional yeast has a nutty, cheesy flavor and is used in countless recipes for cheese sauces, pastas, gravies, tofu and meatless patties.

SESAME SEEDS

They may be tiny, but sesame seeds open up a world of flavors and textures wherever they go. Add toasted sesame seeds to salads, cereals and vegetables. Tahini, a paste made from sesame seeds, is a necessary ingredient in hummus and can also be used as a spread for sandwiches. See below for a tasty, versatile tahini sauce.

SHIITAKE MUSHROOMS

The complex flavor of shiitake mushrooms blends a touch of smoke with a hint of pine and autumn leaves. This rich savoriness (umami) can elevate vegetable or grain dishes to gourmet status.

WALNUTS

Along with a delectable flavor and delicious crunch, walnuts provide a good source of hard-to-get omega-3 fatty acids. Add them to pancake batters, cookies, breads and salads. Because they are high in protein and fiber, walnuts also make a satisfying snack.

VEGAN "PARMESAN"

Combine equal parts almonds or cashews, nutritional yeast and bread crumbs in a food processor. Season with a pinch of garlic powder. Pulse to combine and add salt to taste. Use as a topping for pizza, salad or vegetables.

TAHINI SAUCE

Whisk ½ cup tahini, ¼ cup lemon juice, ¼ cup olive oil, plus minced garlic, cumin, salt and pepper in small bowl. Add water to thicken to desired consistency. Serve with falafel or steamed veggies.

BREAKFAST,
SMOOTHIES & JUICES

AVOCADO TOAST

½ cup thawed frozen peas

2 teaspoons lemon juice

1 teaspoon minced fresh tarragon

¼ teaspoon plus ⅛ teaspoon salt, divided

⅛ teaspoon black pepper

1 teaspoon olive oil

1 tablespoon pepitas (raw pumpkin seeds)

4 slices hearty whole grain bread, toasted

1 avocado

1. Combine peas, lemon juice, tarragon, ¼ teaspoon salt and pepper in small food processor; pulse until blended but still chunky. Or combine all ingredients in small bowl and mash with fork to desired consistency.

2. Heat oil in small saucepan over medium heat. Add pepitas; cook and stir 1 to 2 minutes or until toasted. Transfer to small bowl; stir in remaining ⅛ teaspoon salt.

3. Spread about 1 tablespoon pea mixture over each slice of bread. If making one serving, place the remaining pea mixture in a jar or container and store in the refrigerator for a day or two.

4. Cut avocado in half lengthwise around pit. If making one serving, wrap the half with the pit in plastic wrap and store in the refrigerator for one day. Cut the avocado into slices in the shell; use a spoon to scoop the slices out of the shell. Arrange the slices on the toast; top with toasted pepitas.

Makes 2 servings

PECAN WAFFLES

6 tablespoons boiling water

2 tablespoons ground
flaxseed

2¼ cups all-purpose flour

3 tablespoons sugar

1 tablespoon baking powder

½ teaspoon salt

2 cups plain unsweetened
almond milk or soymilk

¼ cup vegetable oil

¾ cup chopped pecans,
toasted*

Vegan buttery spread and
maple syrup for serving

*To toast pecans, spread in single layer
in heavy skillet. Cook over medium heat
2 to 3 minutes or until lightly browned,
stirring frequently.

1. Combine boiling water and flaxseed in small bowl. Let stand until cool. Preheat classic round waffle iron; grease lightly.

2. Whisk flour, sugar, baking powder and salt in large bowl. Whisk almond milk and oil in medium bowl until well blended. Add to flour mixture with flaxseed mixture; stir just until blended. Stir in pecans.

3. For each waffle, pour about ½ cup batter into waffle iron. Close lid and bake until steaming stops. Serve with spread and maple syrup.

Makes 8 waffles

SCRAMBLED TOFU AND POTATOES

POTATOES

- ¼ **cup olive oil**
- 4 **red potatoes, cubed**
- ½ **white onion, sliced**
- 1 **tablespoon chopped fresh rosemary**
- 1 **teaspoon coarse salt**

SCRAMBLED TOFU

- ¼ **cup nutritional yeast**
- ½ **teaspoon ground turmeric**
- 2 **tablespoons water**
- 2 **tablespoons soy sauce**
- 1 **package (about 14 ounces) firm tofu**
- 2 **teaspoons olive oil**
- ½ **cup chopped green bell pepper**
- ½ **cup chopped red onion**

1. For potatoes, preheat oven to 450°F. Pour ¼ cup oil into 12-inch cast iron skillet; place skillet in oven 10 minutes to heat.

2. Bring large saucepan of water to a boil. Add potatoes; cook 5 to 7 minutes or until tender. Drain and return to saucepan; stir in white onion, rosemary and salt. Spread mixture in preheated skillet. Bake 25 to 30 minutes or until potatoes are browned, stirring every 10 minutes.

3. For tofu, combine nutritional yeast and turmeric in small bowl. Stir in water and soy sauce until smooth.

4. Cut tofu into large cubes. Gently squeeze out water; loosely crumble tofu into medium bowl. Heat 2 teaspoons oil in large skillet over medium-high heat. Add bell pepper and red onion; cook and stir 2 minutes or until soft but not browned. Add tofu; drizzle with 3 tablespoons nutritional yeast sauce. Cook and stir about 5 minutes or until liquid is evaporated and tofu is heated through. Stir in additional sauce for stronger flavor, if desired.

5. Divide potatoes among four serving plates; top with tofu mixture.

Makes 4 servings

SUPER OATMEAL

2 cups water

2¾ cups old-fashioned oats

½ cup finely diced dried figs

½ cup sliced almonds, toasted*

⅓ cup packed dark brown sugar

¼ cup flaxseeds

½ teaspoon salt

½ teaspoon ground cinnamon

2 cups plain unsweetened almond milk or other dairy-free milk, plus additional for serving

To toast almonds, spread in single layer in heavy skillet. Cook over medium heat 2 to 3 minutes or until lightly browned, stirring frequently.

1. Bring water to a boil in large saucepan over high heat. Stir in oats, figs, almonds, brown sugar, flaxseeds, salt and cinnamon. Add 2 cups almond milk; mix well.

2. Reduce heat to medium. Cook and stir 5 to 7 minutes or until oatmeal is thick and creamy. Spoon into individual bowls. Serve with additional almond milk, if desired.

Makes 4 to 6 servings

BUTTERMILK PANCAKES

2 cups plain unsweetened soymilk or other dairy-free milk

2 tablespoons lemon juice

2 tablespoons vegetable oil

1 tablespoon agave nectar or maple syrup

1 cup all-purpose flour

1 cup spelt or whole wheat flour

1 teaspoon baking soda

1 teaspoon baking powder

½ teaspoon salt

1 to 2 tablespoons vegan buttery spread, melted or vegetable oil

Fresh fruit and/or maple syrup

1. Combine soymilk and lemon juice in large measuring cup or medium bowl. Set aside 5 minutes. Stir in oil and agave.

2. Whisk all-purpose flour, spelt flour, baking soda, baking powder and salt in large bowl. Whisk in soymilk mixture until fairly smooth. (Some lumps will remain.)

3. Heat large nonstick skillet or griddle over medium-high heat. Brush lightly with melted spread. Pour batter into skillet in 4-inch circles. Cook 3 to 5 minutes or until edges of pancakes become dull and bubbles form on tops. Flip pancakes; cook 1 to 2 minutes or until browned. Keep warm. Serve with fruit and/or maple syrup.

Makes about 14 pancakes

MAPLE PECAN GRANOLA

¼ cup maple syrup, plus additional for serving

¼ cup packed dark brown sugar

1½ teaspoons vanilla

½ teaspoon ground cinnamon

½ teaspoon coarse salt

6 tablespoons vegetable or olive oil

3 cups old-fashioned oats

1½ cups pecans, coarsely chopped

¾ cup shredded coconut

¼ cup ground flaxseed

¼ cup water

Plain dairy-free yogurt or milk (optional)

1. Preheat oven to 350°F. Line sheet pan with parchment paper.

2. Whisk ¼ cup maple syrup, brown sugar, vanilla, cinnamon, salt and oil in large bowl. Stir in oats, pecans, coconut and flaxseed until evenly coated. Stir in water. Spread mixture evenly on prepared sheet pan, pressing into even layer.

3. Bake 30 minutes or until mixture is golden brown and fragrant. Cool completely on sheet pan. Serve with yogurt and additional maple syrup, if desired. Store leftovers in an airtight container at room temperature 1 month.

Makes about 6 cups

NOTE: For chunky granola, do not stir during baking. For loose granola, stir every 10 minutes during baking.

FRENCH TOAST STICKS

1 cup vanilla soymilk

3 tablespoons all-purpose flour

½ teaspoon ground cinnamon

½ teaspoon vanilla

1 rectangular loaf unsliced French bread (16 ounces)

1 to 2 tablespoons vegan buttery spread

Powdered sugar

Maple syrup

1. Whisk soymilk, flour, cinnamon and vanilla in large bowl.

2. Cut bread into 12 (4×1×1-inch) pieces.

3. Melt 1 tablespoon spread on large nonstick griddle or in large skillet over medium-high heat. Dip bread sticks in soymilk mixture to coat. Cook sticks about 5 minutes until golden brown on all sides, adding additional spread if needed. Dust lightly with powdered sugar and serve with maple syrup.

Makes 4 servings

FRUITY WHOLE-GRAIN CEREAL

2 cups water

½ teaspoon salt

¼ cup uncooked quick-cooking pearl barley

¼ cup uncooked instant brown rice or whole grain brown rice

½ cup plain unsweetened soymilk or almond milk

⅓ cup golden raisins

¼ cup finely chopped dried dates

¼ cup chopped dried plums

¼ cup old-fashioned oats

¼ cup oat bran

2 tablespoons packed brown sugar

½ teaspoon ground cinnamon

1. Bring water and salt to a boil in medium saucepan. Add barley and rice. Reduce heat to low; cover and simmer 8 minutes.

2. Stir in soymilk, raisins, dates, plums, oats, oat bran, brown sugar and cinnamon. Cover and simmer 10 minutes or until mixture is creamy and grains are al dente, stirring once. Serve hot. Refrigerate any leftover cereal in airtight container.

Makes 6 servings

TIP: To reheat cereal, place one serving in microwavable bowl. Microwave 30 seconds; stir. Add water or dairy-free milk for desired consistency. Microwave just until hot.

ORCHARD CRUSH JUICE

2 apples
1 cup fresh raspberries
1 cup fresh strawberries

Juice apples, raspberries and strawberries. Stir.

Makes 2 servings

TOFU PEANUT BUTTER SMOOTHIE

1 banana, cut into chunks
4 ounces silken or soft tofu
¼ cup creamy peanut butter
2 tablespoons agave nectar *or* 1 tablespoon sugar
1 teaspoon vanilla
1 to 2 ice cubes

1. Place all ingredients in blender. Blend 15 to 30 seconds or until smooth, pulsing to break up ice.

2. Pour into glass; serve immediately.

Makes 1 serving

TANGERAPPLE JUICE

2 apples
2 tangerines, peeled
¼ lemon, peeled

Juice apples, tangerines and lemon. Stir.

Makes 2 servings

DOUBLE GREEN PINEAPPLE JUICE

4 leaves Swiss chard
4 leaves kale
¼ pineapple, peeled

Juice chard, kale and pineapple. Stir.

Makes 1 serving

SHARP APPLE COOLER

3 apples
1 cucumber
¼ cup fresh mint
1 inch fresh ginger, peeled

Juice apples, cucumber, mint and ginger. Stir.

Makes 3 servings

BERRY SOY-CREAM BLEND

2 cups frozen mixed berries
1 can (14 ounces) blackberries with juice
1 cup soymilk or almond milk
1 cup apple juice
4 ounces silken or soft tofu

1. Combine berries, soymilk, apple juice and tofu in blender. Blend 15 to 30 seconds or until smooth.

2. Pour into glasses. Serve immediately.

Makes 2 servings

MELONADE

¼ seedless watermelon, rind removed

1 apple

1 lemon, peeled

Juice watermelon, apple and lemon. Stir.

Makes 4 servings

TOFU, FRUIT AND VEGGIE SMOOTHIE

1 cup frozen pineapple chunks

4 ounces silken or soft tofu

½ cup apple juice

½ cup orange juice

1 container (about 2½ ounces) baby food carrots

1. Combine pineapple, tofu, apple juice, orange juice and carrots in blender. Process 15 to 30 seconds or until smooth, pulsing to break up chunks.

2. Pour into glasses. Serve immediately.

Makes 2 servings

CUCUMBER BASIL COOLER

1 cucumber
1 apple
½ cup fresh basil
½ lime, peeled

Juice cucumber, apple, basil and lime. Stir.

Makes 2 servings

TOFU ORANGE DREAM

4 ounces silken or soft tofu
½ cup orange juice
1 container (about 2½ ounces) baby food carrots
2 tablespoons agave nectar *or* 1 tablespoon sugar
¼ teaspoon grated fresh ginger
2 to 3 ice cubes

1. Combine tofu, orange juice, carrots, agave, ginger and ice in blender. Blend 15 to 30 seconds or until smooth, pulsing to break up chunks.

2. Pour into glass. Serve immediately.

Makes 1 serving

MORNING JUICE BLEND

¼ pineapple, peeled

1 orange, peeled

1 inch fresh ginger, peeled

Juice pineapple, orange and ginger. Stir.

Makes 2 servings

PEANUT BUTTER BANANA BLEND

1 frozen banana

½ cup dairy-free yogurt

½ cup almond milk or soymilk

1 tablespoon peanut butter

Banana slices (optional)

1. Combine all ingredients except banana slices in blender; blend 15 to 30 seconds or until smooth, pulsing to break up chunks.

2. Pour into glasses. Garnish with banana slices.

Makes 2 servings

SNACKS,
SMALL BITES & BREADS

CURLY CURRY CHIPS

4 small or 2 large russet
  potatoes, peeled
1 teaspoon vegetable oil
¾ teaspoon salt, divided
1 tablespoon olive oil
¼ cup finely chopped onion
1 tablespoon all-purpose flour
1 tablespoon curry powder
1 cup vegetable broth

1. Preheat oven to 450°F. Line large baking sheet with parchment paper.

2. Spiral potatoes with thick spiral blade of spiralizer. Spread potatoes on prepared baking sheet; drizzle with vegetable oil. Bake 30 to 35 minutes or until golden brown and crispy, turning once. Sprinkle with ½ teaspoon salt.

3. Heat olive oil in small saucepan over medium-high heat. Add onion; cook and stir about 3 minutes or until softened. Whisk in flour and curry powder until well blended; cook 1 minute, stirring constantly. Add broth in thin steady stream, whisking constantly.

4. Reduce heat to medium; cook about 10 minutes or until thick. Taste and add ¼ teaspoon salt, if desired. For smoother sauce, cool slightly and purée in blender or food processor. Serve with potatoes.

Makes 4 servings

NOTE: If you don't have a spiralizer, make regular oven fries instead. Peel potatoes and cut lengthwise into ¼-inch strips. Place in colander; rinse under cold water 2 minutes. Pat dry with paper towels. Toss with 2 teaspoons oil in medium bowl until coated. Spread in single layer on baking sheet. Bake about 25 minutes or until golden brown and crisp, turning once.

FRIED TOFU WITH SESAME DIPPING SAUCE

3 tablespoons soy sauce or tamari

2 tablespoons unseasoned rice vinegar

2 teaspoons sugar

1 teaspoon sesame seeds, toasted*

1 teaspoon dark sesame oil

⅛ teaspoon red pepper flakes

1 package (about 14 ounces) extra firm tofu

¼ cup all-purpose flour

¼ cup rice milk or plain unsweetened soymilk

1 tablespoon cornstarch

¾ cup panko bread crumbs

4 tablespoons vegetable oil

To toast sesame seeds, spread seeds in small skillet. Shake skillet over medium-low heat about 3 minutes or until seeds begin to pop and turn golden.

1. For dipping sauce, combine soy sauce, vinegar, sugar, sesame seeds, sesame oil and red pepper flakes in small bowl. Set aside.

2. Drain tofu and press between paper towels to remove excess water. Cut crosswise into four slices; cut each slice diagonally into triangles. Place flour in shallow dish. Stir rice milk into cornstarch in shallow bowl until smooth. Place panko in another shallow bowl.

3. Dip each piece of tofu in flour to lightly coat all sides; dip in rice milk mixture, turning to coat. Drain and let excess drip back into bowl; roll in panko to coat.

4. Heat 2 tablespoons vegetable oil in large nonstick skillet over high heat. Reduce heat to medium; add half of tofu in single layer. Cook 1 to 2 minutes per side or until golden brown. Repeat with remaining tofu. Serve with dipping sauce.

Makes 4 servings

SOCCA (FARINATA)

1 cup chickpea flour

¾ teaspoon salt

½ teaspoon black pepper

1 cup water

5 tablespoons olive oil, divided

1½ teaspoons minced fresh basil *or* ½ teaspoon dried basil

1 teaspoon minced fresh rosemary *or* ¼ teaspoon dried rosemary

¼ teaspoon dried thyme

1. Sift chickpea flour into medium bowl. Stir in salt and pepper. Gradually whisk in water until smooth. Stir in 2 tablespoons oil. Let stand at least 30 minutes.

2. Preheat oven to 450°F. Place 9- or 10-inch cast iron skillet in oven to heat.

3. Add basil, rosemary and thyme to batter; whisk until smooth. Carefully remove skillet from oven. Add 2 tablespoons oil to skillet, swirling to coat pan evenly. Immediately pour in batter.

4. Bake 12 to 15 minutes or until edge of pancake begins to pull away from side of pan and center is firm. Remove from oven. Preheat broiler.

5. Brush with remaining 1 tablespoon oil. Broil 2 to 4 minutes or until dark brown in spots. Cut into wedges. Serve warm.

Makes 6 servings

TIP: Socca are pancakes made of chickpea flour and are commonly served in paper cones as a savory street food in the south of France, especially around Nice.

BEANS AND GREENS CROSTINI

4 tablespoons olive oil, divided

1 small onion, thinly sliced

4 cups thinly sliced Italian black kale or other dinosaur kale variety

2 tablespoons minced garlic, divided

1 tablespoon balsamic vinegar

2 teaspoons salt, divided

¼ teaspoon red pepper flakes

1 can (about 15 ounces) cannellini beans, rinsed and drained

1 tablespoon chopped fresh rosemary

Toasted baguette slices

1. Heat 1 tablespoon oil in large skillet over medium heat. Add onion; cook and stir 5 minutes or until softened. Add kale and 1 tablespoon garlic; cook 15 minutes or until kale is softened and most liquid has evaporated, stirring occasionally. Stir in vinegar, 1 teaspoon salt and red pepper flakes.

2. Meanwhile, combine beans, remaining 3 tablespoons oil, 1 tablespoon garlic, 1 teaspoon salt and rosemary in food processor or blender; process until smooth.

3. Spread bean mixture over toast and top with kale.

Makes about 24 crostini

ONION FRITTERS WITH RAITA

8 ounces seedless cucumber (about 8 inches)

½ cup vegan sour cream

1 clove garlic, minced

2 teaspoons chopped fresh mint

1 teaspoon salt, divided

½ cup chickpea flour

½ teaspoon baking powder

¼ teaspoon ground cumin

1 tablespoon minced fresh cilantro

¼ cup water

2 yellow or sweet onions (8 ounces each), thinly sliced

½ cup vegetable oil

1. For sauce, shred cucumber with large holes of box grater. Combine sour cream, garlic, mint and ½ teaspoon salt in medium bowl. Stir in cucumber. Refrigerate until ready to use.

2. For fritters, whisk chickpea flour, baking powder, remaining ½ teaspoon salt and cumin in large bowl. Stir in cilantro. Whisk in water in thin steady stream until batter is the consistency of heavy cream. Add additional water by teaspoons if batter is too thick. Stir in onions until coated with batter.

3. Heat oil in large cast iron skillet over medium-high heat (the oil is ready when a drop of batter sizzles). Working in batches, drop level ¼ cupfuls of onion mixture into hot oil. Cook about 2 minutes or until bottoms are well browned. Turn and press lightly with spatula. Cook 2 minutes or until well browned on both sides. Drain on paper towels. Serve hot with sauce.

Makes 10 fritters and 1¼ cups sauce

EXOTIC VEGGIE CHIPS

3 tropical tubers (malanga, yautia, lila and/or taro roots)*

1 to 2 yellow (unripe) plantains

2 parsnips, peeled

1 medium sweet potato, peeled

1 lotus root,** peeled

Vegetable oil for deep frying

Coarse salt

*These tropical tubers are all similar and their labels are frequently interchangeable or overlapping. They are available in the produce sections of Latin markets. Choose whichever tubers are available and fresh. Look for firm roots without signs of mildew or soft spots.

**Lotus root is available in the produce sections of Asian markets. The outside looks like a fat beige link sausage, but when sliced, the lacy, snowflake-like pattern inside is revealed.

1. Line two baking sheets with paper towels. Peel thick shaggy skin from tubers, rinse and dry. Cut tubers into 3-inch lengths.

2. Slice tubers with slicing blade of food processor, mandoline or sharp knife and place in single layer on prepared baking sheets to absorb excess moisture. (Stack in multiple layers with paper towels between layers.) Peel thick skin from plantain. Slice and arrange on paper towels. Slice parsnips and sweet potato and transfer to paper towels. Trim lotus root and remove tough skin with paring knife; slice and transfer to paper towels.

3. Fill deep fryer or deep heavy saucepan with about 3 tablespoons oil and heat over medium-high heat to 350°F. Working in batches, deep fry each vegetable until crisp and slightly curled, stirring occasionally. Frying time will vary from 2 to 6 minutes depending on the vegetable. Remove vegetables with slotted spoon and drain on paper towels; immediately sprinkle with salt. Return oil to 350°F after each batch.

4. Once drained and cooled, combine chips in large bowl. Serve at once or store in airtight containers at room temperature. To recrisp chips, bake in preheated 350°F oven 5 minutes.

Makes about 6 servings

SPICY ROASTED CHICKPEAS

1 can (about 15 ounces) chickpeas, rinsed and drained

3 tablespoons olive oil

½ teaspoon salt

½ teaspoon black pepper

¾ to 1 tablespoon chili powder

⅛ to ¼ teaspoon ground red pepper

1 lime, cut into wedges

1. Preheat oven to 400°F.

2. Combine chickpeas, oil, salt and black pepper in large bowl; toss to coat. Spread in single layer on sheet pan.

3. Bake 15 minutes or until chickpeas begin to brown, shaking pan twice.

4. Sprinkle with chili powder and red pepper. Bake 5 minutes or until dark golden-red. Serve with lime wedges.

Makes 4 servings

BLACK BEAN SLIDERS

6 tablespoons boiling water

2 tablespoons ground flaxseed

1 can (15 ounces) black beans, rinsed and drained

2 cloves garlic

¼ teaspoon salt

½ cup chopped onion

½ cup chopped red bell pepper

2 tablespoons chopped fresh parsley

1 cup plain dry bread crumbs

2 tablespoons vegetable oil

32 mini whole wheat pita breads, cut in half horizontally

Sliced avocado and salsa (optional)

1. Combine boiling water and flaxseed in small bowl. Let stand until cool.

2. Preheat oven to 375°F. Spray baking sheet with nonstick cooking spray.

3. Combine flaxseed mixture, beans, garlic and salt in food processor or blender; process just until smooth. Add onion, bell pepper and parsley; pulse until combined. Stir in bread crumbs.

4. Shape mixture into 32 (1-inch) patties. Place on prepared baking sheet. Brush patties lightly with oil.

5. Bake 10 minutes. Turn over; bake 10 minutes or until firm and heated through. Serve in pitas with avocado and salsa, if desired.

Makes 32 mini sliders

BRUSCHETTA

4 plum tomatoes, seeded and diced

½ cup packed fresh basil leaves, finely chopped

5 tablespoons olive oil, divided

2 cloves garlic, minced

2 teaspoons finely chopped oil-packed sun-dried tomatoes

¼ teaspoon salt

⅛ teaspoon black pepper

16 slices Italian bread

1. Combine fresh tomatoes, basil, 3 tablespoons oil, garlic, sun-dried tomatoes, salt and pepper in large bowl; mix well. Let stand at room temperature 1 hour for flavors to blend.

2. Preheat oven to 375°F. Place bread on baking sheet. Brush remaining 2 tablespoons oil over one side of each bread slice. Bake 6 to 8 minutes or until toasted.

3. Top each bread slice with 1 tablespoon tomato mixture.

Makes 1 cup (8 servings)

TORTILLA CUPS WITH CORN AND BLACK BEAN SALAD

3 tablespoons vegetable oil, divided

1 teaspoon salt, divided

½ teaspoon chili powder

6 (6-inch) flour tortillas

1 cup corn

1 cup chopped red bell pepper

1 cup canned black beans, rinsed and drained

1 small ripe avocado, diced

¼ cup lime juice

¼ cup chopped fresh cilantro

1 small jalapeño pepper, seeded and minced

1. Preheat oven to 350°F. Spray 6 standard (2½-inch) muffin cups with nonstick cooking spray. Whisk 1 tablespoon oil, ½ teaspoon salt and chili powder in small bowl until well blended.

2. Stack tortillas; wrap loosely in waxed paper. Microwave on HIGH 10 to 15 seconds or just until softened. Brush one side of each tortilla lightly with oil mixture; press into prepared cups, oiled side up.

3. Bake about 10 minutes or until edges are golden brown. Cool in pan 2 minutes; remove to wire rack to cool completely.

4. Combine corn, bell pepper, beans and avocado in large bowl. Whisk remaining 2 tablespoons oil, ½ teaspoon salt, lime juice, cilantro and jalapeño in small bowl until well blended. Add to corn mixture; toss gently to coat. Fill tortilla cups with salad. Serve immediately. (Tortilla cups and salad can be prepared ahead of time; fill cups just before serving.)

Makes 6 servings

TIP: For slightly larger tortilla cups, use the back of the muffin pan instead. Spray the back of a 12-cup muffin pan with nonstick cooking spray. Soften the tortillas and brush with the oil mixture, then fit them between the cups on the back of the muffin pan. (Only about three will fit at one time, so two batches are required.) Bake at 350°F about 8 minutes or until edges are golden brown.

SOFT GARLIC BREADSTICKS

1½ cups water

6 tablespoons olive oil

4 cups all-purpose flour

2 tablespoons sugar

1 package (¼ ounce) active dry yeast

1½ teaspoons salt

¾ teaspoon coarse salt

¼ teaspoon garlic powder

1. Heat water and 2 tablespoons oil in small saucepan or microwavable bowl to 110° to 115°F.

2. Combine flour, sugar, yeast and 1½ teaspoons salt in large bowl of stand mixer; beat on low speed to combine. Add water mixture; beat until dough begins to come together. Knead on low speed with dough hook about 5 minutes or until dough is smooth and elastic. Shape dough into a ball. Place in large greased bowl; turn to grease top. Cover and let rise in warm place about 1 hour or until doubled in size.

3. Line two baking sheets with parchment paper or spray with nonstick cooking spray. Punch down dough. For each breadstick, pull off piece of dough slightly larger than a golf ball (about 2 ounces) and roll between hands or on work surface into 7-inch-long stick. Place on prepared baking sheets; cover loosely and let rise in warm place about 45 minutes or until doubled in size.

4. Preheat oven to 400°F. Brush breadsticks with 2 tablespoons oil; sprinkle with coarse salt.

5. Bake breadsticks 13 to 15 minutes or until golden brown. Stir garlic powder into remaining 2 tablespoons oil; brush over breadsticks immediately after removing from oven. Serve warm.

Makes about 16 breadsticks

CREAMY CASHEW SPREAD

1 cup raw cashews

2 tablespoons lemon juice

1 tablespoon tahini

½ teaspoon salt

½ teaspoon black pepper

2 teaspoons minced fresh
   herbs, such as basil,
   parsley or oregano
   (optional)

Crackers

1. Rinse cashews and place in medium bowl. Cover with water by at least 2 inches. Soak 4 hours or overnight. Drain cashews, reserving soaking water.

2. Place cashews, 2 tablespoons reserved water, lemon juice, tahini, salt and pepper in food processor or blender; process several minutes or until smooth. Add additional water, 1 tablespoon at a time, until desired consistency is reached.

3. Cover and refrigerate until ready to serve. Stir in herbs, if desired, just before serving. Serve with crackers.

Makes about ½ cup

TIP: Use this dip as a spread for sandwiches or as a pasta topping. Thin it with additional liquid as needed. You can also use it in place of sour cream as a topping for tacos and chili.

SCALLION PANCAKES

2¼ cups all-purpose flour, divided

1 teaspoon sugar

⅔ cup boiling water

¼ to ½ cup cold water

2 teaspoons dark sesame oil

½ cup finely chopped green onion tops

1 teaspoon coarse salt

½ to ¾ cup vegetable oil

1. Combine 2 cups flour and sugar in large bowl. Stir in boiling water and mix with chopsticks or fork just until water is absorbed and mixture forms large clumps. Gradually stir in enough cold water until dough forms a ball and is no longer sticky.

2. Place dough on lightly floured surface; flatten slightly. Knead dough 5 minutes or until smooth and elastic. Wrap dough with plastic wrap; let stand 1 hour.

3. Knead dough briefly on lightly floured surface; divide dough into four pieces. Roll one piece into 6- to 7-inch round, keeping remaining pieces wrapped in plastic wrap to prevent drying out. Brush dough with ½ teaspoon sesame oil; sprinkle evenly with 2 tablespoons green onions and ¼ teaspoon salt. Roll up into tight cylinder.

4. Coil cylinder into a spiral and pinch end under into dough. Repeat with remaining dough pieces, sesame oil, green onions and salt. Cover with plastic wrap and let stand 15 minutes.

5. Roll each coiled piece of dough into 6- to 7-inch round on lightly floured surface with floured rolling pin.

6. Heat ½ cup vegetable oil in wok over medium-high heat to 375°F; adjust heat to maintain temperature. Carefully place one pancake into hot oil. Fry 2 to 3 minutes per side or until golden. While pancake is frying, press center lightly with metal spatula to ensure even cooking. Drain on paper towels. Repeat with remaining pancakes, adding additional oil if necessary. Cut into wedges; serve immediately.

Makes 32 wedges

PITA BREAD

4½ cups all-purpose flour
1 tablespoon salt
1 tablespoon sugar
1 package (¼ ounce) rapid-rise active dry yeast (2¼ teaspoons)
1½ cups warm water (120°F)
3 tablespoons olive oil

1. Combine 4 cups flour, salt, sugar and yeast in large bowl; whisk until well blended. Add water and oil; stir with wooden spoon until rough dough forms. If dough appears too dry, add additional 1 to 2 tablespoons water. Knead on lightly floured surface 5 to 7 minutes or until dough is smooth and elastic. Or attach dough hook to stand mixer; knead on low speed about 5 minutes or until dough is smooth and elastic. Grease large bowl with olive oil or nonstick cooking spray. Place dough in bowl; turn to grease top. Cover with plastic wrap; let rise in warm place 1 hour or until doubled in size.

2. Turn out dough onto work surface; press into circle. Cut dough into 6 or 8 wedges. Roll each wedge into a smooth ball. Flatten slightly. Let stand 10 minutes for gluten to relax. Roll each ball into circle about ¼ inch thick.

3. Preheat oven to 500°F. Place sheet pan upside down on oven rack; heat 10 minutes. Place 3 or 4 dough rounds on baking sheet. Bake 5 minutes or until pitas are puffed and set but not browned. Repeat with remaining dough rounds. Cool on wire rack.

Makes 6 to 8 pita breads

CLASSIC HUMMUS

1 can (20 ounces) chickpeas, drained
¾ cup tahini
¼ cup cold water
¼ cup lemon juice
2 cloves garlic
1 teaspoon salt
  Olive oil for serving
  Aleppo pepper or paprika

1. Combine chickpeas, tahini, water, lemon juice, garlic and salt in food processor; process 5 minutes until hummus is fluffy and very smooth.

2. Spread in serving bowl; drizzle with oil and sprinkle with pepper.

Makes about 2½ cups

QUINOA PATTIES WITH ROASTED RED PEPPER SAUCE

1 cup uncooked quinoa

2 cups water

1½ teaspoons salt, divided

¾ cup boiling water

¼ cup ground flaxseed

1 jar (12 ounces) roasted red peppers, drained

1 tablespoon balsamic vinegar

1 teaspoon lemon juice

1 teaspoon sugar

1 clove garlic

1 cup plain dry bread crumbs

⅓ cup nutritional yeast

2 tablespoons chopped fresh parsley

2 cloves garlic, minced

½ teaspoon Italian seasoning

1 to 2 tablespoons olive oil

1. Place quinoa in fine-mesh strainer; rinse well under cold running water.

2. Bring 2 cups water, quinoa and ½ teaspoon salt to a boil in medium saucepan over high heat. Reduce heat to low; cover and simmer 10 to 15 minutes or until quinoa is tender and water is absorbed. Cool slightly.

3. Combine boiling water and flaxseed in small bowl. Let stand until cool.

4. Meanwhile, blend roasted peppers, vinegar, lemon juice, sugar, whole garlic clove and ½ teaspoon salt in blender or food processor until smooth. Set aside.

5. Combine quinoa, flaxseed mixture, bread crumbs, nutritional yeast, parsley, minced garlic, Italian seasoning and remaining ½ teaspoon salt in large bowl. Shape into 12 large patties or 24 small patties.

6. Heat 1 tablespoon oil in large skillet over medium heat. Add 6 patties; cook 5 to 7 minutes or until bottoms are browned. Flip patties; cook 5 to 7 minutes or until browned on bottoms. Repeat with remaining patties, adding additional 1 tablespoon oil, if necessary. Serve patties with red pepper sauce.

Makes 6 servings

BARBECUE SEITAN SKEWERS

1 package (8 ounces) seitan, cubed

½ cup barbecue sauce, divided

1 red bell pepper, cut into 12 pieces

1 green bell pepper, cut into 12 pieces

12 cremini mushrooms

1 zucchini, cut into 12 pieces

1. Place seitan in medium bowl. Add ¼ cup barbecue sauce; stir to coat. Marinate in refrigerator 30 minutes. Soak eight 6-inch or four 8-inch bamboo skewers in water 20 minutes.

2. Oil grid. Prepare grill for direct cooking. Thread seitan, bell peppers, mushrooms and zucchini onto skewers.

3. Grill skewers, covered, over medium-high heat 8 minutes or until seitan is hot and glazed with sauce, brushing with some of remaining sauce and turning occasionally.

Makes 4 to 8 servings

SALADS
& VEGETABLES

FATTOUSH SALAD

2 pita breads

⅓ cup plus 3 tablespoons olive oil, divided

Salt and black pepper

2 cups chopped romaine or green leaf lettuce

1 seedless cucumber, quartered lengthwise and sliced

2 tomatoes, diced

4 green onions, thinly sliced

3 radishes, thinly sliced

1 tablespoon finely chopped fresh mint

¼ cup finely chopped fresh parsley

2 tablespoons pomegranate molasses

2 cloves garlic, minced

2 tablespoons red wine vinegar

1 tablespoon lemon juice

1. Preheat oven to 400°F. Cut pita bread into 1-inch pieces. Toss with 3 tablespoons oil and ½ teaspoon salt in large bowl. Spread on large baking sheet. Bake 10 minutes or until pita pieces are browned and crisp. Cool completely on baking sheet.

2. Combine lettuce, cucumber, tomatoes, green onions, radishes, mint and parsley in large bowl. Add pita pieces.

3. For dressing, combine remaining ⅓ cup oil, pomegranate molasses, garlic, vinegar and lemon juice in small bowl. Season with ½ teaspoon salt and pepper; whisk until well blended. Taste and adjust seasoning. Pour over salad; toss until well blended and ingredients are coated.

Makes 4 to 6 servings

CRUNCHY ORANGE-GINGER SLAW

1 package (3 ounces) ramen noodles, any flavor, coarsely crumbled*

1 tablespoon sesame seeds

6 cups finely shredded green cabbage

2 cups shredded carrots

½ cup diced red onion

½ cup raisins

¾ cup orange marmalade, microwaved for 30 seconds

¼ cup cider vinegar

¼ cup canola oil

3 tablespoons grated fresh ginger

1 tablespoon soy sauce

1 teaspoon grated orange peel (optional)

1 teaspoon hot pepper sauce *or* ¼ teaspoon red pepper flakes

½ teaspoon salt

Discard seasoning packet.

1. Heat medium skillet over medium-high heat. Add noodles and sesame seeds; cook 2 minutes or until lightly browned, stirring frequently. Set aside on plate.

2. Combine cabbage, carrots, onion and raisins in large bowl. Whisk marmalade, vinegar, oil, ginger, soy sauce, orange peel, if desired, hot pepper sauce and salt in medium bowl until well blended. Add to cabbage mixture; mix well. Cover and refrigerate at least 20 minutes.

3. Sprinkle with toasted noodles and sesame seed mixture before serving.

Makes 6 to 8 servings

TEXAS CAVIAR

1 tablespoon vegetable oil

1 cup fresh corn (from 2 to 3 ears)

3 cups cooked black-eyed peas*

1 can (15 ounces) black beans

1 cup halved grape tomatoes

1 bell pepper (red, orange, yellow or green), finely chopped

½ cup finely chopped red onion

1 jalapeño pepper, seeded and minced

2 green onions, minced

¼ cup chopped fresh cilantro

2 tablespoons red wine vinegar

1 tablespoon plus 1 teaspoon lime juice, divided

1 teaspoon salt

1 teaspoon sugar

½ teaspoon ground cumin

½ teaspoon dried oregano

2 cloves garlic, minced

¼ cup olive oil

Use 2 (15-ounce) cans, rinsed and drained or cook the beans from dried. Soak 8 ounces of dried beans in salted water at least 4 hours or overnight. Drain beans and place in large saucepan. Cover with water and bring to a boil over high heat. Reduce heat; simmer 45 minutes to 1 hour or until beans are tender. Drain and cool.

1. Heat vegetable oil in large skillet over high heat. Add corn; cook and stir about 3 minutes or until corn is beginning to brown in spots. Place in large bowl. Add beans, tomatoes, bell pepper, onion, jalapeño, green onions and cilantro.

2. Combine vinegar, 1 tablespoon lime juice, salt, sugar, cumin, oregano and garlic in small bowl. Whisk in olive oil in thin steady stream until well blended. Pour over vegetables; stir to coat.

3. Refrigerate at least 2 hours or overnight. Just before serving, stir in remaining 1 teaspoon lime juice. Taste and season with additional salt, if desired.

Makes about 9 cups

NOTE: Serve Texas Caviar as a dip for a crowd with corn chips or tortilla chips. It also makes a great packable lunch or side dish.

CURRIED CAULIFLOWER AND BRUSSELS SPROUTS

2 pounds cauliflower florets

12 ounces brussels sprouts, cut in half lengthwise

⅓ cup olive oil

2 tablespoons curry powder

1 teaspoon salt

½ teaspoon black pepper

½ cup chopped fresh cilantro

1. Preheat oven to 400°F. Line sheet pan with foil or spray with nonstick cooking spray.

2. Combine cauliflower, brussels sprouts and oil in large bowl; toss to coat. Sprinkle with curry powder, salt and pepper; toss to coat. Spread in single layer on prepared pan.

3. Roast 20 to 25 minutes or until golden brown, stirring once halfway through roasting. Transfer to serving bowl; sprinkle with cilantro.

Makes 6 to 8 servings

TOASTED PEANUT COUSCOUS SALAD

1 cup water

1 teaspoon salt, divided

½ cup uncooked couscous

1 cup finely chopped red onion

1 green bell pepper, finely chopped

½ cup dry-roasted peanuts

2 tablespoons soy sauce

1½ tablespoons cider vinegar

1 tablespoon dark sesame oil

1 teaspoon grated fresh ginger

2 teaspoons sugar

⅛ teaspoon red pepper flakes

1. Bring water and ½ teaspoon salt to a boil in small saucepan over high heat. Remove from heat; stir in couscous. Cover tightly and let stand 5 minutes or until water is absorbed. Fluff with fork and transfer to medium bowl; cool slightly. Stir in onion and bell pepper.

2. Heat small nonstick skillet over medium-high heat. Add peanuts; cook 2 to 3 minutes or until beginning to turn golden, stirring frequently. Add to couscous.

3. Whisk soy sauce, vinegar, oil, ginger, sugar, remaining ½ teaspoon salt and red pepper flakes in small bowl. Add to couscous; stir until well blended.

Makes 4 servings

SWEET AND SAVORY SWEET POTATO SALAD

4 cups cubed peeled cooked sweet potatoes (4 to 6)

¾ cup chopped green onions

½ cup chopped fresh parsley

½ cup dried tart cherries

¼ cup plus 2 tablespoons rice wine vinegar

2 tablespoons coarse mustard

1 tablespoon olive oil

1 clove garlic, minced

½ teaspoon salt

¼ teaspoon black pepper

1. Combine sweet potatoes, green onions, parsley and cherries in large bowl; gently mix.

2. Whisk vinegar, mustard, oil, garlic, salt and pepper in small bowl until well blended. Pour over sweet potato mixture; stir gently to coat. Serve immediately or cover and refrigerate until ready to serve.

Makes 6 servings

NOTE: You can cook the sweet potatoes in boiling water or in the oven. Peel the potatoes and cut them into ½- to 1-inch cubes. To boil them, bring a large saucepan of water to a boil; add 1 tablespoon salt. Add potatoes; cook about 10 minutes or until tender. To roast the potatoes, toss them with 1 tablespoon olive oil and a pinch of salt in medium bowl. Preheat oven to 400°F. Spread potatoes on sheet pan. Roast 25 to 30 minutes or until tender, stirring once or twice.

WHEAT BERRY APPLE SALAD

1 cup uncooked wheat berries
   (whole wheat kernels)

1 teaspoon salt, divided

2 apples (1 red and 1 green)

½ cup dried cranberries

⅓ cup chopped walnuts

1 stalk celery, chopped

   Grated peel and juice of
   1 medium orange

2 tablespoons rice wine
   vinegar

1½ tablespoons chopped fresh
   mint

1 tablespoon olive oil

   Lettuce leaves (optional)

1. Place wheat berries and ½ teaspoon salt in large saucepan; cover with 1 inch of water.* Bring to a boil. Stir and reduce heat to low. Cover; cook 45 minutes to 1 hour or until wheat berries are tender but chewy, stirring occasionally. Add additional water if wheat berries become dry during cooking. Drain and let cool. Wheat berries can be cooked up to 4 days in advance. Refrigerate until ready to use.

2. Cut apples into bite-size pieces. Combine wheat berries, apples, cranberries, walnuts, celery, orange peel, orange juice, vinegar, mint, oil and remaining ½ teaspoon salt in large bowl. Cover; refrigerate at least 1 hour to allow flavors to blend. Serve on lettuce leaves, if desired.

To cut cooking time by 20 to 30 minutes, wheat berries may be soaked in water overnight. Drain and cover with 1 inch fresh water before cooking.

Makes 4 to 6 servings

BARLEY WITH CURRANTS AND PINE NUTS

1 tablespoon olive oil

1 onion, finely chopped

2 cups vegetable broth

½ cup uncooked pearl barley

⅓ cup currants

½ teaspoon salt

¼ teaspoon black pepper

¼ cup pine nuts

1. Heat oil in medium saucepan over medium-high heat. Add onion; cook 5 minutes or until lightly browned, stirring occasionally. Add broth, barley, currants, salt and pepper; bring to a boil. Reduce heat to low.

2. Cover and simmer 30 minutes or until barley is tender and broth is absorbed. Stir in pine nuts; serve immediately.

Makes 4 servings

GREEK SALAD WITH TOFU "FETA"

TOFU "FETA"

- 1 package (about 14 ounces) firm or extra firm tofu
- ½ cup extra virgin olive oil
- ¼ cup lemon juice
- 2 teaspoons salt
- 2 teaspoons Greek or Italian seasoning
- ½ teaspoon black pepper
- 1 teaspoon onion powder
- ½ teaspoon garlic powder

SALAD

- 1 pint grape tomatoes, halved
- 2 seedless cucumbers, quartered lengthwise and sliced
- 1 yellow bell pepper, slivered
- 1 small red onion, cut in thin slices

1. For "feta," cut tofu crosswise into two pieces, each about 1 inch thick. Place on cutting board lined with paper towels; top with layer of paper towels. Place weighted baking dish on top of tofu. Let stand 30 minutes to drain. Pat tofu dry and crumble into large bowl.

2. Combine oil, lemon juice, salt, Greek seasoning and black pepper in small jar with lid; shake until well blended. Reserve ¼ cup mixture for salad dressing. Add onion powder and garlic powder to remaining mixture; pour over tofu and toss gently. Cover and refrigerate 2 hours or overnight.

3. For salad, combine tomatoes, cucumbers, bell pepper and onion in serving bowl. Add tofu and reserved dressing. Toss gently.

Makes 4 to 6 servings

ROASTED VEGETABLE SALAD WITH CAPERS AND WALNUTS

1 pound small brussels sprouts, trimmed

1 pound unpeeled small Yukon Gold potatoes, cut into halves

½ teaspoon salt

¼ teaspoon black pepper

¼ teaspoon dried rosemary

5 tablespoons olive oil, divided

1 red bell pepper, cut into bite-size pieces

¼ cup walnuts, coarsely chopped

2 tablespoons capers, drained

1½ tablespoons white wine vinegar

1. Preheat oven to 400°F.

2. Slash bottoms of brussels sprouts; place in shallow roasting pan. Add potatoes; sprinkle with salt, black pepper and rosemary. Drizzle with 3 tablespoons oil; toss to coat. Roast 20 minutes. Stir in bell pepper; roast 15 minutes or until tender. Transfer to large bowl; stir in walnuts and capers.

3. Whisk remaining 2 tablespoons oil and vinegar in small bowl until blended. Pour over salad; toss to coat. Serve at room temperature.

Makes 6 to 8 servings

CARAMELIZED BRUSSELS SPROUTS WITH CRANBERRIES

1 tablespoon vegetable oil

1 pound brussels sprouts, ends trimmed, thinly sliced

¼ cup dried cranberries

2 teaspoons packed brown sugar

¼ teaspoon salt

1. Heat oil in large skillet over medium–high heat. Add brussels sprouts; cook 10 minutes or until crisp–tender and beginning to brown, stirring occasionally.

2. Add cranberries, brown sugar and salt; cook and stir 5 minutes or until brussels sprouts are browned.

Makes 4 servings

BALSAMIC BUTTERNUT SQUASH

3 tablespoons olive oil

2 tablespoons thinly sliced fresh sage (about 6 large leaves), divided

1 medium butternut squash, peeled and cut into 1-inch pieces (4 to 5 cups)

½ red onion, cut in half and cut into ¼-inch slices

1 teaspoon salt, divided

2½ tablespoons balsamic vinegar

¼ teaspoon black pepper

1. Heat oil in large (12-inch) cast iron skillet over medium-high heat. Add 1 tablespoon sage; cook and stir 3 minutes. Add squash, onion and ½ teaspoon salt; cook 6 minutes, stirring occasionally. Reduce heat to medium; cook 15 minutes without stirring.

2. Stir in vinegar, remaining ½ teaspoon salt and pepper; cook 10 minutes or until squash is tender, stirring occasionally. Stir in remaining 1 tablespoon sage; cook 1 minute.

Makes 4 servings

GREEN BEANS WITH GARLIC-CILANTRO SAUCE

1½ pounds green beans, trimmed

3 tablespoons olive oil

1 red bell pepper, cut into thin strips

½ sweet onion, halved and thinly sliced

2 teaspoons minced garlic

1 teaspoon salt

2 tablespoons chopped fresh cilantro

Black pepper

1. Bring large saucepan of salted water to a boil over medium-high heat. Add beans; cook 6 minutes or until tender. Drain and return to saucepan.

2. Meanwhile, heat oil in large skillet over medium-high heat. Add bell pepper and onion; cook and stir 3 minutes or until vegetables are tender but not browned. Add garlic; cook and stir 30 seconds. Add beans and salt; cook and stir 2 minutes or until beans are heated through and coated. Stir in cilantro; season with black pepper. Serve immediately.

Makes 4 to 6 servings

COLORFUL COLESLAW

¼ head green cabbage,
   shredded or thinly sliced

¼ head red cabbage,
   shredded or thinly sliced

1 small yellow or orange bell
   pepper, thinly sliced

1 small jicama, peeled and
   julienned

¼ cup thinly sliced green
   onions

2 tablespoons chopped fresh
   cilantro

¼ cup vegetable oil

¼ cup fresh lime juice

1 teaspoon salt

⅛ teaspoon black pepper

1. Combine cabbage, bell pepper, jicama, green onions and cilantro in large bowl.

2. Whisk oil, lime juice, salt and black pepper in small bowl until well blended. Pour over vegetables; toss to coat. Cover and refrigerate 2 to 6 hours for flavors to blend.

Makes 4 to 6 servings

NOTE: This coleslaw makes a great topping for tacos and sandwiches.

ROASTED SWEET POTATO AND APPLE SALAD

2 large sweet potatoes, peeled and cubed

2 tablespoons olive oil, divided

¾ teaspoon salt, divided

¼ teaspoon black pepper

3 tablespoons apple juice

1 tablespoon balsamic vinegar

1 tablespoon Dijon mustard

1 tablespoon maple syrup

2 teaspoons snipped fresh chives

1 medium Gala apple, diced (about 1 cup)

½ cup finely chopped celery

¼ cup thinly sliced red onion

Lettuce leaves (optional)

1. Preheat oven to 450°F. Place sweet potatoes on sheet pan. Drizzle with 1 tablespoon oil and sprinkle with ¼ teaspoon salt and pepper; toss to coat and spread in single layer.

2. Roast 25 to 30 minutes or until potatoes are tender, stirring halfway through cooking time. Cool completely.

3. Meanwhile, whisk remaining 1 tablespoon oil, apple juice, vinegar, mustard, maple syrup, chives and remaining ½ teaspoon salt in small bowl until smooth and well blended.

4. Combine sweet potatoes, apple, celery and onion in medium bowl. Drizzle with dressing; gently toss to coat. Serve on lettuce leaves, if desired.

Makes 4 servings

QUINOA AND ROASTED CORN

1 cup uncooked quinoa

2 cups water

½ teaspoon salt

4 ears corn *or* 2 cups frozen corn

¼ cup plus 1 tablespoon vegetable oil, divided

1 cup chopped green onions, divided

1 teaspoon coarse salt

1 cup quartered grape tomatoes or chopped plum tomatoes, drained*

1 cup black beans, rinsed and drained

Juice of 1 lime (about 2 tablespoons)

¼ teaspoon grated lime peel

¼ teaspoon sugar

¼ teaspoon ground cumin

¼ teaspoon black pepper

Place tomatoes in fine-mesh strainer and place over bowl 10 to 15 minutes.

1. Place quinoa in fine-mesh strainer; rinse well under cold running water. Combine quinoa, 2 cups water and salt in medium saucepan; bring to a boil over high heat. Reduce heat to low; cover and simmer 15 to 18 minutes or until quinoa is tender and water is absorbed. Transfer to large bowl.

2. Meanwhile, remove husks and silk from corn; cut kernels off cobs. Heat ¼ cup oil in large skillet over medium-high heat. Add corn; cook 10 to 12 minutes or until tender and lightly browned, stirring occasionally. Stir in ⅔ cup green onions and coarse salt; cook and stir 2 minutes. Add corn mixture to quinoa. Gently stir in tomatoes and beans.

3. Combine lime juice, lime peel, sugar, cumin and pepper in small bowl. Whisk in remaining 1 tablespoon oil until blended. Pour over quinoa mixture; toss lightly to coat. Sprinkle with remaining ⅓ cup green onions. Serve warm or chilled.

Makes 6 to 8 servings

CRISPY SKILLET POTATOES

2 tablespoons olive oil

4 red potatoes, cut into
   wedges

½ cup chopped onion

2 tablespoons lemon-pepper
   seasoning

½ teaspoon coarse salt

   Chopped fresh parsley
   (optional)

1. Heat oil in large cast iron skillet over medium heat. Stir in potatoes, onion, lemon-pepper seasoning and salt. Cover and cook 25 to 30 minutes or until potatoes are tender and browned, turning occasionally.

2. Sprinkle with parsley just before serving.

Makes 4 servings

CHOPPED SALAD WITH CORNBREAD CROUTONS

½ loaf cornbread (recipe follows), cut into 1-inch cubes

1 large sweet potato, peeled and cut into 1-inch pieces

5 tablespoons olive oil, divided

1½ teaspoons salt, divided

3 tablespoons red wine vinegar

2 tablespoons white wine vinegar

1 tablespoon maple syrup

1 clove garlic, minced

1 teaspoon dry mustard

⅛ teaspoon dried oregano

Pinch red pepper flakes

½ cup vegetable oil

1 head iceberg lettuce

1 cup halved grape tomatoes

2 green onions, thinly sliced

1 avocado, diced

½ cup coarsely chopped smoked almonds

½ cup dried cranberries

1. Preheat oven to 400°F. Prepare cornbread. Cool in baking dish at least 10 minutes or cool completely; remove to cutting board. Cut half of cornbread into 1-inch cubes when cool enough to handle. Return to baking dish. *Reduce oven temperature to 350°F.* Bake 10 to 12 minutes or until cornbread is dry and toasted.

2. Spread sweet potato in 13×9-inch baking pan. Drizzle with 1 tablespoon olive oil and sprinkle with ½ teaspoon salt; toss to coat. Bake 30 to 35 minutes or until browned and tender, stirring once or twice. Cool completely.

3. For dressing, whisk vinegars, maple syrup, garlic, mustard, oregano, red pepper flakes and remaining 1 teaspoon salt in medium bowl; whisk in remaining 4 tablespoons olive oil and vegetable oil in thin steady stream.

4. Remove outer lettuce leaves and core. Chop lettuce into ½-inch pieces and place in large bowl. Add tomatoes, green onions and half of dressing; mix well. Add sweet potato, avocado, almonds and cranberries; mix well. Taste and add additional dressing, if desired. Add croutons; mix gently.

Makes 6 to 8 servings

CORNBREAD

3 tablespoons boiling water

1 tablespoon ground flaxseed

1¼ cups all-purpose flour

¾ cup yellow cornmeal

⅓ cup sugar

2 teaspoons baking powder

1 teaspoon salt

1¼ cups plain unsweetened soymilk or almond milk

¼ cup vegetable oil

1. Preheat oven to 400°F. Spray 8-inch square baking dish or pan with nonstick cooking spray. Combine boiling water and flaxseed in small bowl; let stand 5 minutes or until cooled and thickened.

2. Combine flour, cornmeal, sugar, baking powder and salt in large bowl; mix well. Whisk soymilk and oil in medium bowl until well blended. Add to flour mixture with flaxseed mixture; stir just until dry ingredients are moistened. Pour batter into prepared baking dish.

3. Bake about 25 minutes or until golden brown and toothpick inserted into center comes out clean.

Makes 9 to 12 servings

QUINOA TABBOULEH

1 cup uncooked tricolor quinoa *or* ½ cup *each* red and white quinoa

2 cups water

2 teaspoons salt, divided

2 cups chopped tomatoes (red, orange or a combination)

1 cucumber, quartered lengthwise and thinly sliced

¼ cup olive oil

3 tablespoons fresh lemon juice

½ teaspoon black pepper

1 red or orange bell pepper, chopped

½ cup minced fresh parsley

1. Rinse quinoa in fine-mesh strainer under cold water. Combine 2 cups water, quinoa and 1 teaspoon salt in medium saucepan. Bring to a boil over high heat. Reduce heat to low; cover and simmer 10 to 15 minutes until quinoa is tender and water is absorbed. Transfer to large bowl; cool to room temperature.

2. Meanwhile, combine tomatoes, cucumber and remaining 1 teaspoon salt in medium bowl. Let stand 20 minutes.

3. Stir cucumbers, tomatoes, cucumbers and any accumulated juices into quinoa. Whisk oil, lemon juice and black pepper in same medium bowl until well blended. Stir into quinoa mixture. Add bell pepper and parsley; mix until well blended. Taste and season with additional salt and pepper, if desired.

Makes 6 to 8 servings

NOTE: For a heartier dish, add some chickpeas. Drain a 15-ounce can of chickpeas and rinse under cold water. Stir into quinoa with bell pepper.

PERSIMMON AND CHICKPEA SALAD

1 can (15 ounces) chickpeas, rinsed and drained

2 tablespoons olive oil, divided

½ teaspoon salt, divided

¼ teaspoon black pepper

¼ cup tahini

2 tablespoons lemon juice

2 tablespoons maple syrup

2 tablespoons water

2 cups microgreens

1 head radicchio, chopped

2 persimmons, thinly sliced

2 avocados, thinly sliced

½ cup pomegranate seeds

¼ cup pecan halves, toasted

1 blood orange, cut into wedges (optional)

1. Preheat oven to 400°F.

2. Combine chickpeas, 1 tablespoon oil, ¼ teaspoon salt and pepper in large bowl; toss to coat. Spread in single layer in 13×9-inch baking pan.

3. Bake 15 minutes or until chickpeas begin to brown, shaking pan twice.

4. For dressing, whisk tahini, remaining 1 tablespoon oil, lemon juice, maple syrup, 2 tablespoons water and remaining ¼ teaspoon salt in small bowl.

5. Arrange greens, radicchio, persimmons, avocados, pomegranate seeds and pecans in serving bowls. Add chickpeas and drizzle with dressing. Garnish with orange wedges.

Makes 4 servings

VEGETABLE AND NUT ROAST

6 tablespoons boiling water

2 tablespoons ground flaxseed

1½ cups unsalted walnuts, pecans, almonds or cashews

2 tablespoons olive oil

1 onion, finely chopped

4 ounces cremini mushrooms (about 6 large), sliced

2 cloves garlic, minced

1 can (about 14 ounces) diced tomatoes

1 cup old-fashioned oats

2 tablespoons all-purpose flour

1 tablespoon chopped fresh sage

1 tablespoon chopped fresh parsley

1 teaspoon chopped fresh thyme

Salt and black pepper

1. Preheat oven to 350°F. Spray 8×4-inch loaf pan with nonstick cooking spray. Combine boiling water and flaxseed in small bowl. Let stand until cool.

2. Place nuts in food processor. Pulse until finely chopped, allowing some larger pieces to remain. Transfer to large bowl.

3. Heat oil in medium skillet over medium heat. Add onion, mushrooms and garlic; cook and stir 3 minutes or until softened. Transfer mixture to bowl with nuts.

4. Stir in flaxseed mixture, tomatoes, oats, flour, sage, parsley, thyme, salt and pepper until combined. Spoon mixture into prepared pan. Bake 45 to 50 minutes or until firm and browned. Cool slightly before slicing.

Makes 6 to 8 servings

SOUPS,
STEWS & CHILIES

BLACK BEAN SOUP

2 tablespoons vegetable oil

1 cup diced onion

1 stalk celery, diced

2 carrots, diced

½ small green bell pepper, diced

4 cloves garlic, minced

4 cans (15 ounces each) black beans, rinsed and drained, divided

4 cups (32 ounces) vegetable broth, divided

2 tablespoons cider vinegar

2 teaspoons chili powder

½ teaspoon salt

½ teaspoon ground red pepper

½ teaspoon ground cumin

¼ teaspoon liquid smoke

Optional toppings: vegan sour cream, chopped green onions and vegan cheese shreds

1. Heat oil in large saucepan or Dutch oven over medium-low heat. Add onion, celery, carrots, bell pepper and garlic; cook 10 minutes, stirring occasionally.

2. Combine half of beans and 1 cup broth in food processor or blender; process until smooth. Add to vegetables in saucepan.

3. Stir in remaining beans, remaining broth, vinegar, chili powder, salt, red pepper, cumin and liquid smoke; bring to a boil over high heat. Reduce heat to medium-low; cook 1 hour or until vegetables are tender and soup is thickened. Serve with desired toppings.

Makes 4 to 6 servings

GARDEN VEGETABLE SOUP

1 tablespoon olive oil

1 medium onion, chopped

1 carrot, chopped

1 stalk celery, chopped

1 medium zucchini, diced

1 medium yellow squash, diced

1 red bell pepper, diced

2 tablespoons tomato paste

2 cloves garlic, minced

2 teaspoons salt

1 teaspoon Italian seasoning

½ teaspoon black pepper

8 cups vegetable broth

1 can (28 ounces) whole tomatoes, chopped, juice reserved

½ cup uncooked pearl barley

1 cup cut green beans (1-inch pieces)

½ cup corn

¼ cup slivered fresh basil

1 tablespoon lemon juice

1. Heat oil in large saucepan or Dutch oven over medium-high heat. Add onion, carrot and celery; cook and stir 8 minutes or until vegetables are softened. Add zucchini, yellow squash and bell pepper; cook and stir 5 minutes or until softened. Stir in tomato paste, garlic, salt, Italian seasoning and black pepper; cook 1 minute. Stir in broth and tomatoes with juice; bring to a boil. Stir in barley.

2. Reduce heat to low; cook 30 minutes. Stir in green beans and corn; cook about 15 minutes or until barley is tender and green beans are crisp-tender. Stir in basil and lemon juice.

Makes 8 to 10 servings

JAMAICAN BLACK BEAN STEW

2 cups uncooked brown rice

2 pounds sweet potatoes

3 pounds butternut squash

1 tablespoon olive oil

1 large onion, coarsely chopped

3 cloves garlic, minced

1 tablespoon curry powder

1½ teaspoons ground allspice

1 teaspoon salt

½ teaspoon ground red pepper

1 can (about 14 ounces) vegetable broth *or* 1¾ cups water

2 cans (15 ounces each) black beans, rinsed and drained

½ cup raisins

3 tablespoons fresh lime juice

1 cup diced tomato

1 cup diced peeled cucumber

1. Prepare rice according to package directions. Meanwhile, peel sweet potatoes; cut into ¾-inch chunks to measure 4 cups. Peel squash; remove seeds. Cut into ¾-inch cubes to measure 5 cups.

2. Heat oil in Dutch oven over medium-high heat. Add onion; cook and stir 5 minutes or until tender. Add garlic, curry powder, allspice, salt and red pepper; cook and stir 30 seconds. Add broth, sweet potatoes and squash. Bring to a boil over high heat. Reduce heat to low; cover and simmer 15 minutes or until sweet potatoes and squash are tender. Add beans and raisins; simmer 5 minutes or until heated through. Stir in lime juice.

3. Serve stew over rice; top with tomato and cucumber.

Makes 8 servings

WHITE BEANS AND TOMATOES

1 pound dried cannellini beans, soaked 8 hours or overnight

2 tablespoons olive oil

2 medium onions, chopped

1 tablespoon minced garlic

1 tablespoon tomato paste

4 teaspoons dried oregano

2 teaspoons salt

1 can (28 ounces) crushed tomatoes

2 cups water

Black pepper (optional)

1. Drain and rinse beans. Heat oil in large saucepan over medium-high heat. Add onions; cook and stir 5 to 7 minutes or until tender and lightly browned. Add garlic, tomato paste, oregano and salt; cook and stir 1 minute. Stir in beans, tomatoes and water; mix well.

2. Reduce heat to low. Cover and simmer 1 hour or until beans are tender, stirring occasionally. Season with black pepper, if desired.

Makes 8 to 10 servings

PASTA E CECI

4 tablespoons olive oil, divided

1 onion, chopped

1 carrot, chopped

1 clove garlic, minced

1 fresh rosemary sprig

1 teaspoon salt

1 can (15 ounces) chickpeas, undrained

2 cups vegetable broth or water

1 can (28 ounces) whole tomatoes, drained and crushed

1 bay leaf

⅛ teaspoon red pepper flakes

1 cup uncooked orecchiette

Black pepper

Chopped fresh parsley or basil

1. Heat 3 tablespoons oil in large saucepan over medium-high heat. Add onion and carrot; cook and stir 10 minutes or until vegetables are softened.

2. Add garlic, rosemary and salt; cook and stir 1 minute. Add chickpeas with liquid, broth, tomatoes, bay leaf and red pepper flakes. Remove 1 cup mixture; place in food processor or blender. Process until smooth. Stir back into saucepan; bring to a boil.

3. Add pasta; reduce heat to medium and cook 12 to 15 minutes or until pasta is tender and mixture is creamy. Remove bay leaf and rosemary sprig. Taste and season with additional salt and black pepper, if desired. Divide among bowls; garnish with parsley and drizzle with remaining 1 tablespoon oil.

Makes 4 servings

NOTE: To crush the tomatoes, take them out of the can one at a time and crush them between your fingers over the saucepan. Or coarsely chop them with a knife.

MINESTRONE SOUP

1 tablespoon olive oil

½ cup chopped onion

1 stalk celery, diced

1 carrot, diced

2 cloves garlic, minced

2 cups vegetable broth

1½ cups water

1 bay leaf

¾ teaspoon salt

½ teaspoon dried basil

½ teaspoon dried oregano

¼ teaspoon dried thyme

¼ teaspoon sugar

Ground black pepper

1 can (about 15 ounces) dark red kidney beans, rinsed and drained

1 can (about 15 ounces) navy beans or cannellini beans, rinsed and drained

1 can (about 14 ounces) diced tomatoes

1 cup diced zucchini (about 1 small)

½ cup uncooked small shell pasta

½ cup frozen cut green beans

¼ cup dry red wine

1 cup packed chopped fresh spinach

1. Heat oil in large saucepan or Dutch oven over medium-high heat. Add onion, celery, carrot and garlic; cook and stir 5 to 7 minutes or until vegetables are tender. Add broth, water, bay leaf, salt, basil, oregano, thyme, sugar and pepper; bring to a boil.

2. Stir in kidney beans, navy beans, tomatoes, zucchini, pasta, green beans and wine; cook 10 minutes, stirring occasionally.

3. Add spinach; cook 2 minutes or until pasta and zucchini are tender. Remove and discard bay leaf.

Makes 4 to 6 servings

FOUR-BEAN CHILI

2 tablespoons olive oil

1 onion, finely chopped

2 medium carrots, chopped

1 red bell pepper, chopped

3 tablespoons chili powder

2 tablespoons ground cumin

2 tablespoons tomato paste

2 tablespoons packed dark brown sugar

3 cloves garlic, minced

1 tablespoon dried oregano

1 teaspoon salt

1 can (28 ounces) diced tomatoes

1 can (15 ounces) tomato sauce

1 can (about 15 ounces) small white beans, rinsed and drained

1 can (about 15 ounces) light kidney beans, rinsed and drained

1 can (about 15 ounces) dark kidney beans, rinsed and drained

1 can (about 15 ounces) pinto beans, rinsed and drained

1 cup vegetable broth

1 can (4 ounces) diced mild green chiles

1 ounce unsweetened baking chocolate, chopped

1 tablespoon cider vinegar

1. Heat oil in large saucepan or Dutch oven over medium-high heat. Add onion, carrots and bell pepper; cook 10 minutes or until vegetables are tender, stirring frequently. Add chili powder, cumin, tomato paste, brown sugar, garlic, oregano and salt; cook and stir 1 minute.

2. Stir in tomatoes, tomato sauce, beans, broth, chiles and chocolate; bring to a boil. Reduce heat to medium; simmer 20 minutes, stirring occasionally. Stir in vinegar.

Makes 8 to 10 servings

LENTIL SOUP

2 tablespoons olive oil, divided

2 medium onions, chopped

1½ teaspoons salt

4 cloves garlic, minced

¼ cup tomato paste

1 teaspoon dried oregano

½ teaspoon dried basil

¼ teaspoon dried thyme

¼ teaspoon black pepper

½ cup dry sherry or white wine

8 cups vegetable broth

2 cups water

3 carrots, cut into ½-inch pieces

2 cups dried lentils, rinsed and sorted

1 cup chopped fresh parsley

1 tablespoon balsamic vinegar

1. Heat 1 tablespoon oil in large saucepan or Dutch oven over medium heat. Add onions; cook 10 minutes, stirring occasionally. Add remaining 1 tablespoon oil and salt; cook 10 minutes or until onions are golden brown, stirring frequently.

2. Add garlic; cook and stir 1 minute. Add tomato paste, oregano, basil, thyme and pepper; cook and stir 1 minute. Stir in sherry; cook 30 seconds, scraping up browned bits from bottom of saucepan.

3. Stir in broth, water, carrots and lentils; cover and bring to a boil over high heat. Reduce heat to medium-low; cook, partially covered, 30 minutes or until lentils are tender.

4. Remove from heat; stir in parsley and vinegar.

Makes 6 to 8 servings

RAINBOW VEGETABLE STEW

1 tablespoon olive oil

1 red onion, chopped

2 stalks celery, chopped

3 cloves garlic, minced

2 teaspoons salt, divided

4 cups vegetable broth

1 butternut squash (about 2 pounds), peeled and cut into ½-inch cubes

1 red bell pepper, chopped

1 green bell pepper, chopped

1 teaspoon ground cumin

½ teaspoon dried oregano

¼ teaspoon chipotle chili powder

1½ cups water

¾ cup uncooked tricolor or white quinoa

½ cup corn

1 can (15 ounces) black beans, rinsed and drained

½ cup chopped fresh parsley

1 tablespoon lime juice

1. Heat oil in large saucepan over medium-high heat. Add onion and celery; cook and stir 5 minutes or until vegetables are softened. Add garlic and 1½ teaspoons salt; cook and stir 30 seconds. Stir in broth, squash, bell peppers, cumin, oregano and chipotle chili powder; bring to a boil. Reduce heat to medium; simmer 20 minutes or until squash is tender.

2. Meanwhile, bring 1½ cups water, quinoa and remaining ½ teaspoon salt to a boil in medium saucepan. Reduce heat to low; cover and simmer 15 minutes or until quinoa is tender and water is absorbed.

3. Stir corn and beans into stew; cook 5 minutes or until heated through. Stir in parsley and lime juice. Serve with quinoa.

Makes 4 to 6 servings

WEST AFRICAN PEANUT SOUP

2 tablespoons vegetable oil

1 large onion, chopped

½ cup chopped roasted peanuts

1½ tablespoons minced fresh ginger

4 cloves garlic, minced (about 1 tablespoon)

1 teaspoon salt

4 cups vegetable broth

2 sweet potatoes, peeled and cut into ½-inch cubes

1 can (28 ounces) whole tomatoes, drained and coarsely chopped

¼ teaspoon ground red pepper

1 bunch Swiss chard or kale, stemmed and shredded

⅓ cup unsweetened peanut butter (creamy or chunky)

1. Heat oil in large saucepan over medium-high heat. Add onion; cook and stir 5 minutes or until softened. Add peanuts, ginger, garlic and salt; cook and stir 1 minute. Stir in broth, sweet potatoes, tomatoes and red pepper; bring to a boil. Reduce heat to medium; simmer 10 minutes.

2. Stir in chard and peanut butter; cook over medium-low heat 10 minutes or until vegetables are tender and soup is creamy.

Makes 6 to 8 servings

CREAMY TOMATO SOUP

4 tablespoons olive oil, divided

1 large onion, finely chopped

2 cloves garlic, minced

2 teaspoons sugar

1 teaspoon salt

½ teaspoon dried oregano

2 cans (28 ounces each) peeled Italian plum tomatoes, undrained

4 cups ½-inch focaccia cubes (half of 9-ounce loaf)

½ teaspoon freshly ground black pepper

½ cup canned coconut milk

1. Heat 3 tablespoons oil in large saucepan over medium-high heat. Add onion; cook and stir 5 minutes or until softened. Add garlic, sugar, salt and oregano; cook 30 seconds. Stir in tomatoes with juice; bring to a boil. Reduce heat to medium-low; simmer 45 minutes, stirring occasionally.

2. Meanwhile, preheat oven to 350°F. Combine focaccia cubes, remaining 1 tablespoon oil and pepper in large bowl; toss to coat. Spread on large rimmed baking sheet. Bake about 10 minutes or until bread cubes are golden brown.

3. Blend soup with immersion blender or in batches in food processor or blender.* Stir in coconut milk; heat through. Serve soup topped with croutons.

*Check the instructions that came with your device to make sure it can handle hot liquids. If it can't, cool the soup to room temperature before blending.

Makes 6 servings

RIBOLLITA (TUSCAN BREAD SOUP)

2 tablespoons olive oil

1 onion, halved and thinly sliced

2 stalks celery, diced

1 large carrot, julienned

3 cloves garlic, minced

2 medium zucchini, halved lengthwise and thinly sliced

1 medium yellow squash, halved lengthwise and thinly sliced

1 can (28 ounces) whole tomatoes, undrained

1 can (15 ounces) cannellini beans, rinsed and drained

1½ teaspoons salt

1 teaspoon Italian seasoning

¼ teaspoon black pepper

1 bay leaf

¼ teaspoon red pepper flakes (optional)

4 cups vegetable broth

2 cups water

1 bunch kale, stemmed and coarsely chopped *or* 3 cups thinly sliced cabbage

8 ounces Tuscan or other rustic bread, cubed

1. Heat oil in large saucepan over medium-high heat. Add onion, celery and carrot; cook and stir 5 minutes. Add garlic, zucchini and yellow squash; cook and stir 5 minutes.

2. Add tomatoes with juice, beans, salt, Italian seasoning, black pepper, bay leaf and red pepper flakes, if desired. Add broth and water; bring to a boil. Reduce heat; simmer 15 minutes.

3. Add kale and bread; simmer 10 minutes or until vegetables are tender, bread is soft and soup is thick.

Makes 4 servings

NOTE: This is a great recipe to use a spiralizer if you have one. Use the spiral slicing blade to spiral the zucchini and yellow squash, then cut in half to make half moon slices. Use the thin ribbon blade to spiral the onion and carrot, and then cut into desired lengths.

SANDWICHES,
TACOS & WRAPS

FARRO VEGGIE BURGERS

1½ cups water

½ cup pearled farro or spelt

2 medium potatoes, peeled and quartered

2 to 4 tablespoons canola oil, divided

¾ cup finely chopped green onions

1 cup grated carrots

2 teaspoons grated fresh ginger

2 tablespoons ground almonds (almond meal) or ground walnuts

¼ to ¾ teaspoon salt

¼ teaspoon black pepper

½ cup panko bread crumbs

6 whole wheat hamburger buns

Ketchup and mustard (optional)

1. Combine 1½ cups water and farro in medium saucepan; bring to a boil over high heat. Reduce heat to low; partially cover; cook 25 to 30 minutes or until farro is tender. Drain and cool. (If using spelt, use 2 cups of water and cook until tender.)

2. Meanwhile, place potatoes in large saucepan; cover with water. Bring to a boil; reduce heat and simmer 20 minutes or until tender. Mash potatoes; let stand until cool enough to handle.

3. Heat 1 tablespoon oil in medium skillet over medium-high heat. Add green onions; cook and stir 1 minute. Add carrots and ginger; cover and cook 2 to 3 minutes or until carrots are tender. Transfer to large bowl; cool completely.

4. Add mashed potatoes and farro to carrot mixture. Add almonds, salt and pepper; mix well. Shape mixture into six patties. Spread panko on medium plate; coat patties with panko.

5. Heat 1 tablespoon oil in large nonstick skillet over medium heat. Cook patties about 4 minutes per side or until golden brown, adding additional oil as needed. Serve on buns with desired condiments.

Makes 6 servings

EGGLESS EGG SALAD SANDWICH

1 package (about 14 ounces) firm tofu, drained, pressed* and crumbled

1 stalk celery, finely diced

2 green onions, minced

2 tablespoons minced fresh parsley

¼ cup plus 1 tablespoon vegan mayonnaise

3 tablespoons sweet pickle relish

2 teaspoons fresh lemon juice

1 teaspoon mustard

Salt and black pepper

8 slices whole wheat bread, toasted

1½ cups fresh alfalfa sprouts

8 tomato slices

*See page 12 for instructions on pressing tofu.

1. Combine tofu, celery, green onions and parsley in large bowl. Stir mayonnaise, relish, lemon juice and mustard in small bowl until well blended. Add to tofu mixture; mix well. Season with salt and pepper.

2. Serve salad on toast with alfalfa sprouts and tomato slices.

Makes 4 sandwiches

MUSHROOM TOFU BURGERS

3 tablespoons boiling water

1 tablespoon ground flaxseed

3 teaspoons olive oil, divided

1 package (8 ounces) cremini mushrooms, coarsely chopped

½ medium onion, coarsely chopped

1 clove garlic, minced

7 ounces extra firm tofu, crumbled and frozen

1 cup old-fashioned oats

⅓ cup finely chopped walnuts

½ teaspoon salt

½ teaspoon onion powder

¼ teaspoon dried thyme

6 English muffins, split and toasted

Optional toppings: lettuce, tomato and/or red onion slices

1. Combine boiling water and flaxseed in small bowl. Let stand until cool.

2. Heat 1 teaspoon oil in large nonstick skillet over medium heat. Add mushrooms, onion and garlic; cook and stir 10 minutes or until mushrooms have released most of their juices. Remove from heat; cool slightly.

3. Combine mushroom mixture, tofu, oats, walnuts, flaxseed mixture, salt, onion powder and thyme in food processor or blender; process until combined. (Some tofu pieces may remain). Shape mixture into six ⅓-cup patties.

4. Heat 1 teaspoon oil in same skillet over medium-low heat. Working in batches, cook patties 5 minutes per side. Repeat with remaining oil and patties. Serve burgers on English muffins with lettuce, tomato and red onion, if desired.

Makes 6 servings

SESAME GINGER TOFU BÁHN MÌ

4 ounces peeled daikon radish or 5 medium red radishes

1 large carrot

1 tablespoon sugar

¾ cup unseasoned rice vinegar

1 teaspoon salt

1 clove garlic

1 piece (1 inch) peeled fresh ginger

¼ cup soy sauce

1 tablespoon packed brown sugar

1 tablespoon dark sesame oil

1 package (about 14 ounces) extra firm tofu, drained, pressed and halved crosswise

1 tablespoon vegetable oil

8 ounces seedless cucumber (about 8 inches)

1 large loaf (16 ounces) or 2 small loaves (8 ounces each) soft French bread

¼ cup vegan or regular mayonnaise

Fresh cilantro sprigs

1 jalapeño pepper, sliced into rings

1. Spiral radish and carrot with fine spiral blade of spiralizer. Dissolve sugar in vinegar in 2-cup measuring cup; stir in salt. Measure 1 cup total of carrot and radish; add to vinegar. Let stand at least 1 hour for flavors to blend.

2. Place garlic and ginger in food processor; process until finely chopped. Add soy sauce, brown sugar and sesame oil; blend until smooth. Place tofu in 8-inch square baking dish; pour marinade over tofu. Marinate at room temperature 30 minutes to 1 hour, turning occasionally.

3. Drain tofu, discarding marinade. Heat vegetable oil in large cast iron skillet over high heat. Working in batches, cook tofu 3 to 4 minutes per side or until well browned, adding additional oil if needed. Transfer to paper towel-lined cutting board; let stand until cool enough to handle. Cut into thin slices.

4. Spiral cucumber with large spiral blade. Scoop out some of soft insides of bread. Spread mayonnaise over bottoms of bread; top with tofu, cilantro, cucumber, pickled carrot mixture and jalapeños.

Makes 4 to 8 servings

NOTE: If you don't have a spiralizer, use a julienne peeler to cut the cucumber, radish and carrot, or cut into julienne strips with sharp knife.

CAULIFLOWER TACOS WITH CHIPOTLE CREMA

1 package (8 ounces) sliced cremini mushrooms

4 tablespoons olive oil, divided

1¾ teaspoons salt, divided

1 head cauliflower

1 teaspoon ground cumin

½ teaspoon dried oregano

¼ teaspoon ground coriander

¼ teaspoon ground cinnamon

¼ teaspoon black pepper

½ cup vegan sour cream

2 teaspoons lime juice

½ teaspoon chipotle chili powder

½ cup vegetarian refried beans

8 taco-size flour or corn tortillas

Chopped fresh cilantro (optional)

Pickled Red Onions (recipe follows) or chopped red onion

1. Preheat oven to 400°F. Toss mushrooms with 1 tablespoon oil and ¼ teaspoon salt in large bowl. Spread on small baking sheet.

2. Remove leaves from cauliflower. Remove florets; cut into 1-inch pieces. Place in same large bowl. Add remaining 3 tablespoons olive oil, 1 teaspoon salt, cumin, oregano, coriander, cinnamon and black pepper; mix well. Spread on sheet pan in single layer.

3. Roast cauliflower about 40 minutes or until browned and tender, stirring a few times. Roast mushrooms 20 minutes or until dry and browned, stirring once.

4. For crema, combine sour cream, lime juice, chipotle chili powder and remaining ½ teaspoon salt in small bowl.

5. For each taco, spread 1 tablespoon beans over tortilla; spread 1 teaspoon crema over beans. Top with about 3 mushroom slices and ¼ cup cauliflower. Top with pickled red onions and cilantro, if desired.

Makes 8 tacos (4 servings)

PICKLED RED ONIONS: Thinly slice 1 small red onion; place in large glass jar. Add ¼ cup white wine vinegar or distilled white vinegar, 2 tablespoons water, 1 teaspoon sugar and 1 teaspoon salt. Seal jar; shake well. Refrigerate at least 1 hour or up to 1 week. Makes about ½ cup.

CHICKPEA SALAD

1 can (15 ounces) chickpeas, rinsed and drained

1 stalk celery, chopped

1 dill pickle, chopped (about ½ cup)

¼ cup finely chopped red or yellow onion

⅓ cup vegan mayonnaise

1 teaspoon lemon juice

¼ teaspoon salt

Black pepper (optional)

Whole grain bread

Lettuce and tomato slices (optional)

1. Place chickpeas in medium bowl. Coarsely mash with potato masher, leaving some beans whole.

2. Add celery, pickle and onion; stir to mix. Add mayonnaise and lemon juice; mix well. Taste and add ¼ teaspoon salt or more, if desired. Sprinkle with pepper, if desired; mix well. Serve on bread with lettuce and tomato, if desired.

Makes 2 cups (4 to 6 servings)

LENTIL BURGERS

1 can (about 14 ounces) vegetable broth

1 cup dried lentils, rinsed and sorted

1¼ teaspoons salt, divided

3 tablespoons boiling water

1 tablespoon ground flaxseed

1 small carrot, grated

¼ cup coarsely chopped mushrooms

¼ cup plain dry bread crumbs

3 tablespoons finely chopped onion

2 cloves garlic, minced

1 teaspoon dried thyme

¼ cup chopped seeded cucumber

¼ cup plain vegan sour cream

½ teaspoon dried mint

¼ teaspoon dried dill weed

¼ teaspoon black pepper

Kaiser rolls (optional)

1. Bring broth to a boil in medium saucepan over high heat. Stir in lentils and 1 teaspoon salt; reduce heat to low. Simmer, covered, about 30 minutes or until lentils are tender and liquid is absorbed. Cool to room temperature. Combine boiling water and flaxseed in small bowl; let stand 10 minutes.

2. Place lentils, carrot and mushrooms in food processor or blender; process until finely chopped but not smooth. (Some whole lentils should still be visible.) Stir in bread crumbs, onion, garlic, thyme and flaxseed mixture. Cover and refrigerate 2 to 3 hours.

3. Shape lentil mixture into four (½-inch-thick) patties. Spray large skillet with nonstick cooking spray; heat over medium heat. Cook patties over medium-low heat about 10 minutes or until browned on both sides.

4. Meanwhile for sauce, combine cucumber, sour cream, mint, dill, black pepper and remaining ¼ teaspoon salt in small bowl. Serve burgers on rolls with sauce.

Makes 4 servings

SPINACH VEGGIE WRAP

PICO DE GALLO

- **1 cup finely chopped fresh tomatoes (about 2 small)**
- **½ teaspoon salt**
- **¼ cup chopped white onion**
- **2 tablespoons minced jalapeño pepper (about 1 medium)**
- **2 tablespoons chopped fresh cilantro**
- **1 teaspoon lime juice**

GUACAMOLE

- **2 large ripe avocados**
- **¼ cup finely chopped red onion**
- **2 tablespoons chopped fresh cilantro**
- **2 teaspoons fresh lime juice**
- **½ teaspoon salt**

WRAPS

- **4 whole wheat burrito-size tortillas (about 10 inches)**
- **2 cups fresh baby spinach leaves**
- **1 cup sliced mushrooms**
- **1 cup vegan cheese shreds (optional)**
- **Salsa**

1. For pico de gallo, combine 1 cup tomatoes and ½ teaspoon salt in fine-mesh strainer; set in bowl or sink to drain 15 minutes. Combine drained tomatoes, white onion, jalapeño, 2 tablespoons cilantro and 1 teaspoon lime juice in medium bowl; mix well.

2. For guacamole, scoop avocados into medium bowl. Add red onion, 2 tablespoons cilantro, 2 teaspoons lime juice and ½ teaspoon salt; mash with fork to desired consistency.

3. For wraps, spread ¼ cup guacamole on each tortilla. Layer each with ½ cup spinach, ¼ cup mushrooms, ¼ cup cheese shreds, if desired, and ¼ cup pico de gallo. Roll up; serve with salsa.

Makes 4 servings

SLOPPY JOES

2 cups textured soy protein (TVP)

1¾ cups boiling water

½ cup ketchup

½ cup barbecue sauce

2 tablespoons cider vinegar

1 tablespoon packed brown sugar

1 tablespoon soy sauce

1 teaspoon chili powder

1 tablespoon olive oil

½ cup chopped onion

½ cup chopped carrot

¾ cup water

4 to 6 hamburger or hot dog buns

1. Combine textured soy protein and boiling water in large bowl; let stand 10 minutes.

2. For sauce, combine ketchup, barbecue sauce, vinegar, brown sugar, soy sauce and chili powder in medium bowl.

3. Heat oil in large saucepan over medium-high heat. Add onion and carrot; cook and stir 5 minutes or until vegetables are tender. Stir in sauce mixture; bring to a boil. Stir in reconstituted textured soy protein and ¾ cup water. Reduce heat to low; cover and cook 20 minutes. Serve sloppy joes in buns.

Makes 4 to 6 servings

SEITAN FAJITA WRAPS

1 package (1 ounce) fajita seasoning mix

2 packages (8 ounces each) seitan,* sliced

1 tablespoon vegetable oil

1 red bell pepper, sliced

½ medium onion, sliced

1 package (8 ounces) sliced mushrooms

6 taco-size flour or corn tortillas, warmed

Salsa, guacamole and vegan sour cream (optional)

Seitan is a meat substitute made from wheat gluten. It is high in protein and has a meaty, chewy texture. It can be found in the refrigerated section of large supermarkets and specialty food stores.

1. Dissolve seasoning mix according to package directions. Place seitan in large resealable food storage bag. Pour seasoning mixture over seitan. Seal bag; shake to coat.

2. Heat oil in large skillet. Add bell pepper and onion; cook and stir 4 to 5 minutes or until crisp-tender. Add mushrooms; cook and stir 1 to 2 minutes or until mushrooms are softened. Add seitan and seasoning mixture; cook and stir 1 to 2 minutes or until seitan is heated through and vegetables are coated with seasoning.

3. Divide vegetable mixture evenly among tortillas. Serve with salsa, guacamole and sour cream, if desired.

Makes 6 fajitas

CURRIES,
NOODLES & STIR-FRIES

SZECHUAN COLD NOODLES

8 ounces uncooked vermicelli, broken in half, or Chinese egg noodles

3 tablespoons rice vinegar

3 tablespoons soy sauce

2 tablespoons peanut or vegetable oil

1 clove garlic, minced

1 teaspoon minced fresh ginger

1 teaspoon dark sesame oil

½ teaspoon crushed Szechuan peppercorns or red pepper flakes

¼ cup coarsely chopped fresh cilantro (optional)

¼ cup chopped peanuts

1. Cook noodles according to package directions; drain.

2. Combine vinegar, soy sauce, peanut oil, garlic, ginger, sesame oil and peppercorns in large bowl; mix well. Add hot cooked noodles; toss to coat. Sprinkle with cilantro, if desired, and peanuts. Serve at room temperature or chilled.

Makes 4 servings

SZECHUAN VEGETABLE NOODLES: Add 1 cup chopped peeled cucumber, ½ cup chopped red bell pepper, ½ cup sliced green onions and an additional 1 tablespoon soy sauce.

SOBA STIR-FRY

8 ounces uncooked soba (buckwheat) noodles

1 tablespoon olive oil

2 cups sliced shiitake mushrooms

1 medium red bell pepper, cut into thin strips

2 whole dried red chiles *or* ¼ teaspoon red pepper flakes

1 clove garlic, minced

2 cups shredded napa cabbage

½ cup vegetable broth

2 tablespoons tamari or soy sauce

1 tablespoon rice wine or dry sherry

2 teaspoons cornstarch

1 package (about 14 ounces) firm tofu, drained and cut into 1-inch cubes

   Salt and black pepper

2 green onions, thinly sliced

1. Bring large saucepan of salted water to a boil. Add noodles; return to a boil. Reduce heat to low. Cook 3 minutes or until tender. Drain and rinse under cold water to cool.

2. Heat oil in large nonstick skillet or wok over medium-high heat. Add mushrooms, bell pepper, dried chiles and garlic; cook and stir 3 minutes or until mushrooms are tender. Add cabbage; cover and cook 2 minutes or until cabbage is wilted.

3. Whisk broth, tamari and rice wine into cornstarch in small bowl until smooth. Stir sauce into vegetable mixture. Cook 2 minutes or until sauce is thickened.

4. Stir tofu and noodles into vegetable mixture; toss gently until heated through. Season with salt and black pepper; sprinkle with green onions. Serve immediately.

Makes 4 servings

GREEN CURRY WITH TOFU

1 tablespoon vegetable oil

1 onion, chopped

1 package (about 14 ounces) firm tofu, drained and cut into 1-inch cubes

⅓ cup Thai green curry paste

1 can (about 13 ounces) coconut milk

1 broccoli crown (about 8 ounces), cut into florets

1 cup cut green beans (1-inch pieces)

½ teaspoon salt

1 cup uncooked brown rice, cooked according to package directions

1. Heat oil in large skillet or wok over high heat. Add onion; cook and stir 5 minutes or until onion is soft and lightly browned.

2. Add tofu and curry paste; cook and stir 2 minutes or until curry is fragrant and tofu is coated. Add coconut milk; bring to a boil. Reduce heat to low. Add broccoli and green beans.

3. Cook 20 minutes or until vegetables are tender and sauce is thickened, stirring frequently. Taste and season with salt. Serve over rice.

Makes 2 to 4 servings

ROASTED FENNEL AND SPAGHETTI

2 bulbs fennel, trimmed, cored and sliced ¼ inch thick

2 carrots, peeled and quartered

1 tablespoon plus 2 teaspoons olive oil, divided

Salt and black pepper

1 cup fresh bread crumbs

2 cloves garlic, minced

½ teaspoon grated lemon peel

8 ounces uncooked spaghetti or vermicelli

2 tablespoons fresh lemon juice

2 tablespoons chopped fresh oregano

1. Preheat oven to 400°F. Place fennel and carrots on sheet pan. Drizzle with 1 teaspoon oil and sprinkle with ¼ teaspoon each salt and pepper. Toss to coat; spread in single layer.

2. Bake 30 minutes or until vegetables are tender and well browned, stirring once or twice. When carrots are cool enough to handle, cut diagonally into 1-inch pieces.

3. Meanwhile, heat 1 tablespoon oil in medium skillet over medium heat. Add bread crumbs and garlic; cook and stir about 3 minutes or until bread is toasted. Transfer to small bowl; stir in lemon peel and ¼ teaspoon salt.

4. Cook pasta according to package directions in large saucepan of salted water until al dente. Drain and return to saucepan. Stir in lemon juice and remaining 1 teaspoon oil. Divide pasta among serving bowls. Top with vegetables, bread crumbs and oregano.

Makes 2 to 4 servings

MA PO TOFU

1 package (about 14 ounces) firm tofu, drained and pressed*

2 tablespoons soy sauce

2 teaspoons minced fresh ginger

1 cup vegetable broth, divided

2 tablespoons black bean sauce

1 tablespoon Thai sweet chili sauce

1 tablespoon cornstarch

2 tablespoons vegetable oil

1 green bell pepper, cut into bite-size pieces

2 cloves garlic, minced

1½ cups broccoli florets

¼ cup chopped fresh cilantro (optional)

1 cup uncooked rice, cooked according to package directions

*See page 12 for instructions on pressing tofu.

1. Cut tofu into cubes. Place in shallow dish; sprinkle with soy sauce and ginger.

2. Whisk ¼ cup broth, black bean sauce, chili sauce and cornstarch in small bowl until smooth and well blended; set aside.

3. Heat oil in wok or large skillet over high heat. Add bell pepper and garlic; stir-fry 2 minutes. Add remaining ¾ cup broth and broccoli; bring to a boil. Reduce heat; cover and simmer 3 minutes or until broccoli is crisp-tender.

4. Stir sauce mixture; add to wok. Stir-fry 1 minute or until sauce boils and thickens. Stir in tofu; simmer, uncovered, until heated through. Sprinkle with cilantro, if desired. Serve with rice.

Makes 4 servings

SPINACH-ARTICHOKE LASAGNA

1 tablespoon olive oil

1 cup chopped onion

3 cloves garlic, chopped

¼ cup tomato paste

¼ cup white wine

1 can (28 ounces) crushed tomatoes

1 teaspoon salt

1 teaspoon sugar

1 teaspoon dried oregano

Not-Ricotta (recipe follows)

1 can (14 ounces) artichoke hearts, drained and chopped

1 package (10 ounces) frozen chopped spinach, thawed and squeezed dry

9 no-boil lasagna noodles

2 cups vegan mozzarella cheese shreds

2 roasted bell peppers, chopped

1. For sauce, heat oil in large saucepan over medium-high heat. Add onion; cook and stir 5 minutes or until onion is tender. Add garlic; cook and stir 30 seconds. Stir in tomato paste; cook and stir 1 minute. Stir in wine; cook 30 seconds. Add tomatoes, salt, sugar and oregano; break up tomatoes with spoon. Reduce heat to low; partially cover and simmer 30 minutes.

2. Meanwhile, prepare not-ricotta. Combine artichokes and spinach in small bowl.

3. Preheat oven to 350°F. Spray 13×9-inch baking dish with nonstick cooking spray. Spread ½ cup sauce in dish; arrange three noodles over sauce. Spread half of not-ricotta over noodles; top with artichoke mixture, half of cheese shreds and ½ cup sauce. Repeat layers of noodles and not-ricotta; top with roasted peppers, remaining 3 noodles, sauce and cheese shreds.

4. Cover with greased foil; bake 45 minutes. Remove foil; bake 15 minutes. Let stand 10 minutes before serving.

Makes 8 servings

NOT-RICOTTA: Drain 1 package (about 14 ounces) firm tofu and pat dry. Crumble into large bowl. Add 1 cup silken tofu, ½ cup chopped fresh parsley, 2 teaspoons salt, 2 teaspoons lemon juice, 1 teaspoon sugar and 1 teaspoon black pepper; mix well. Refrigerate until needed. Drain liquid before using.

SUMMER SPAGHETTI

1 pound plum tomatoes,
    coarsely chopped

1 medium onion, chopped

⅓ cup chopped fresh parsley

6 pitted green olives, chopped

2 cloves garlic, minced

2 tablespoons finely shredded
    fresh basil *or* ¾ teaspoon
    dried basil

2 teaspoons drained capers

½ teaspoon paprika

¼ teaspoon dried oregano

1 tablespoon red wine vinegar

½ cup olive oil

1 pound uncooked spaghetti

1. Combine tomatoes, onion, parsley, olives, garlic, basil, capers, paprika and oregano in medium bowl; mix well. Drizzle with vinegar. Add oil; stir until well blended. Cover and refrigerate at least 6 hours or overnight.

2. Cook pasta according to package directions; drain. Toss hot pasta with tomato mixture. Serve immediately.

Makes 4 to 6 servings

COLD PEANUT NOODLES WITH EDAMAME

½ (8-ounce) package brown rice pad thai noodles

3 tablespoons soy sauce

2 tablespoons dark sesame oil

2 tablespoons unseasoned rice vinegar

1 tablespoon sugar

1 tablespoon finely grated fresh ginger

1 tablespoon creamy peanut butter

1 tablespoon sriracha or hot chili sauce

2 teaspoons minced garlic

½ cup thawed frozen shelled edamame

¼ cup shredded carrots

¼ cup sliced green onions

Chopped peanuts (optional)

1. Prepare noodles according to package directions for pasta. Rinse under cold water; drain. Cut noodles into 3-inch lengths. Place in large bowl; set aside.

2. Whisk soy sauce, oil, vinegar, sugar, ginger, peanut butter, sriracha and garlic in small bowl until smooth and well blended.

3. Pour dressing over noodles; toss gently to coat. Stir in edamame and carrots. Cover and refrigerate at least 30 minutes before serving. Top with green onions and peanuts, if desired.

Makes 4 servings

NOTE: Brown rice pad thai noodles can be found in the Asian section of the supermarket. Regular thin rice noodles or whole wheat spaghetti may be substituted.

MUSHROOM GRATIN

4 tablespoons vegan buttery spread or olive oil, divided

1 small onion, minced

1 package (8 ounces) sliced cremini mushrooms

2 cloves garlic, minced

4 cups cooked elbow macaroni, rotini or other pasta

2 tablespoons all-purpose flour

1 cup unsweetened plain soymilk or almond milk

½ teaspoon salt

½ teaspoon black pepper

½ teaspoon dry mustard

½ cup fresh bread crumbs

1 tablespoon olive oil

1. Preheat oven to 350°F. Spray shallow baking dish or casserole with nonstick cooking spray.

2. Melt 2 tablespoons spread in large skillet over medium-high heat. Add onion; cook and stir 2 minutes. Add mushrooms and garlic; cook and stir 6 to 8 minutes or until vegetables are soft. Remove from heat; stir in macaroni.

3. Melt remaining 2 tablespoons spread in medium saucepan over low heat. Whisk in flour; cook and stir 2 minutes without browning. Stir in soymilk. Bring to a boil over medium-high heat, whisking constantly. Reduce heat to maintain a simmer. Add salt, pepper and mustard; whisk 5 to 7 minutes or until sauce thickens.

4. Pour sauce over mushroom mixture in skillet; stir to coat. Spoon into prepared baking dish. Top with bread crumbs; drizzle with oil.

5. Cover and bake 15 minutes. Uncover and bake 10 minutes or until bubbly and browned.

Makes 4 servings

VEGETABLE RICE NOODLE STIR-FRY

½ cup soy sauce

⅓ cup sugar

¼ cup lime juice

2 fresh red Thai chiles *or* 1 large jalapeño pepper,* finely chopped

8 ounces thin rice noodles (rice vermicelli)

¼ cup vegetable oil

8 ounces firm tofu, drained and cut into triangles

1 jicama (8 ounces), peeled and chopped *or* 1 can (8 ounces) sliced water chestnuts, drained

2 medium sweet potatoes (1 pound), peeled and cut into ¼-inch-thick slices

2 large leeks, cut into ¼-inch-thick slices

¼ cup chopped unsalted dry-roasted peanuts

2 tablespoons chopped fresh mint

2 tablespoons chopped fresh cilantro

*Chile peppers can sting and irritate the skin, so wear rubber gloves when handling peppers and do not touch your eyes.

1. Combine soy sauce, sugar, lime juice and chiles in small bowl until well blended; set aside.

2. Place rice noodles in medium bowl. Cover with hot water; let stand 15 minutes or until soft. Drain well; cut into 3-inch lengths.

3. Meanwhile, heat oil in large skillet over medium-high heat. Add tofu; cook 4 minutes per side or until golden brown. Remove with slotted spatula to paper towel-lined baking sheet.

4. Add jicama to skillet; stir-fry 5 minutes or until lightly browned. Remove to baking sheet. Cook sweet potatoes in batches until tender and browned; remove to baking sheet. Add leeks; stir-fry 1 minute; remove to baking sheet.

5. Stir soy sauce mixture; add to skillet. Heat until sugar dissolves. Add noodles; toss to coat. Gently stir in tofu, vegetables, peanuts, mint and cilantro.

Makes 4 servings

PUMPKIN CURRY

1 tablespoon vegetable oil

1 package (about 14 ounces)
firm tofu, drained, patted
dry and cut into 1-inch
cubes

¼ cup Thai red curry paste

2 cloves garlic, minced

1 can (15 ounces) pumpkin
purée

1 can (about 13 ounces)
coconut milk

1 cup vegetable broth or
water

1½ teaspoons salt

1 teaspoon sriracha sauce

4 cups cut-up fresh
vegetables (broccoli,
cauliflower, red bell pepper
and/or sweet potato)

½ cup peas

1 cup uncooked jasmine
rice, cooked according to
package directions

¼ cup shredded fresh basil
(optional)

1. Heat oil in wok or large skillet over high heat. Add tofu; stir-fry 5 minutes or until lightly browned. Add curry paste and garlic; cook and stir 1 minute or until tofu is coated.

2. Add pumpkin, coconut milk, broth, salt and sriracha; bring to a boil. Stir in vegetables. Reduce heat to medium; cover and simmer 20 minutes or until vegetables are tender.

3. Stir in peas; cook 1 minute or until heated through. Serve over rice; top with basil, if desired.

Makes 4 servings

MAC AND CHEEZ

1½ cups uncooked elbow macaroni

1 cup chopped onion

1 cup chopped red or green bell pepper

¾ cup chopped celery

¾ cup nutritional yeast

¼ cup all-purpose flour

1½ teaspoons salt

¼ teaspoon garlic powder

¼ teaspoon onion powder

2 cups unsweetened soymilk or other dairy-free milk

1 teaspoon prepared yellow mustard

3 drops hot pepper sauce

½ teaspoon paprika

1. Preheat oven to 350°F. Spray 12×8-inch baking dish with nonstick cooking spray. Prepare macaroni according to package directions for al dente; add onion, bell pepper and celery during last 5 minutes of cooking. Drain; return to saucepan.

2. Meanwhile, combine nutritional yeast, flour, salt, garlic powder and onion powder in medium saucepan. Whisk in soymilk over medium heat until smooth. Add mustard and hot pepper sauce. Continue whisking 10 minutes or until mixture thickens to desired consistency. Pour over macaroni and vegetables; mix well.

3. Spread mixture in prepared baking dish; sprinkle with paprika. Bake 15 to 20 minutes or until heated through.

Makes 4 to 6 servings

TIP: Try this sauce over vegetables for a creamy side dish, or pour over corn chips for vegan nachos.

FRIED CAULIFLOWER RICE

3 tablespoons soy sauce

1 tablespoon plus 1 teaspoon minced fresh ginger, divided

2 teaspoons packed dark sesame oil

1 teaspoon brown sugar

1 teaspoon rice vinegar

1 package (about 14 ounces) firm tofu, drained and cut into 1-inch cubes

2 tablespoons vegetable oil, divided

1 yellow or sweet onion, chopped

1 carrot, chopped

½ cup frozen peas

2 cloves garlic, minced

1 package (12 ounces) frozen cauliflower rice

1 green onion, thinly sliced

1. Whisk soy sauce, 1 tablespoon ginger, sesame oil, brown sugar and vinegar in small bowl. Place tofu in quart-size resealable food storage bag. Pour marinade over tofu. Seal bag, pressing out as much air as possible. Turn to coat tofu with marinade. Refrigerate 3 hours or overnight.

2. Drain tofu, reserving marinade. Heat 1 tablespoon vegetable oil in large skillet over high heat. Add tofu; stir-fry 3 to 5 minutes or until edges are browned. Transfer to bowl.

3. Heat remaining 1 tablespoon vegetable oil in same skillet. Add yellow onion and carrot; stir-fry 2 minutes or until softened. Add peas, garlic and remaining 1 teaspoon ginger; cook 2 minutes or until peas are hot. Add frozen cauliflower rice and ¼ cup reserved marinade; stir-fry 5 minutes or until heated through. Return tofu to skillet; stir-fry until heated through. Top with green onion.

Makes 4 servings

ROASTED SQUASH WITH TAHINI COUSCOUS

1 butternut squash (about 2½ pounds), peeled and cut into ½-inch cubes

2 tablespoons olive oil, divided

1¾ teaspoons salt, divided

1 package (6 ounces) plain pearled couscous (1 cup)

2¾ cups water, divided

½ cup tahini

1 tablespoon maple syrup

¼ teaspoon smoked paprika

¼ cup chopped preserved lemon

Chopped almonds (optional)

Minced fresh parsley (optional)

1. Preheat oven to 400°F. Toss squash, 1 tablespoon oil and 1 teaspoon salt in medium bowl; spread on sheet pan. Bake 30 minutes or until squash is tender and browned, stirring once or twice.

2. Heat remaining 1 tablespoon oil in medium skillet over high heat. Add couscous; cook and stir 2 to 3 minutes or until some of couscous is lightly browned. Stir in ½ teaspoon salt. Add 2½ cups water; bring to a boil. Reduce heat to medium; cook about 10 minutes or until water is mostly absorbed, stirring occasionally. Remove from heat. Cover and let stand 5 minutes or until water is absorbed and couscous is tender.

3. Whisk tahini, maple syrup, paprika and remaining ¼ teaspoon salt in small bowl. Whisk in remaining ¼ cup water until smooth. Stir into couscous. Add squash and preserved lemon; stir gently. Garnish with almonds and parsley. Serve warm.

Makes 4 to 6 servings

NOTE: Butternut squash is notoriously difficult to peel. To make the job easier, invest in a high-quality Y-shaped peeler. Cut a thin slice off the bottom of the squash to give it stability and place it upright on a cutting board. Make downward strokes with the peeler and remove the outer layer of skin. Go over the whole thing a second time until the squash looks bright orange.

CILANTRO PEANUT PESTO ON SOBA

1 cup packed fresh basil leaves

½ cup packed fresh cilantro

¾ cup dry roasted peanuts, divided

1 jalapeño pepper, seeded

3 cloves garlic

2 teaspoons liquid aminos or soy sauce

1 tablespoon plus ¾ teaspoon salt, divided

½ cup peanut oil

1 package (about 12 ounces) uncooked soba noodles

Chopped fresh cilantro

1. Combine basil, ½ cup cilantro, ½ cup peanuts, jalapeño, garlic, liquid aminos and ¾ teaspoon salt in food processor; pulse until coarsely chopped. With motor running, drizzle in oil in thin steady stream; process until well blended.

2. Bring large saucepan of water to a boil. Add remaining 1 tablespoon salt; stir until dissolved. Add noodles; return to a boil. Reduce heat to low. Cook 3 minutes or until tender. Drain and rinse under cold water to cool.

3. Place noodles in medium bowl. Stir in pesto. Chop remaining ¼ cup peanuts; sprinkle over noodles. Garnish with chopped cilantro.

Makes 4 to 6 servings (1 cup pesto)

PESTO FETTUCCINE

1 pound uncooked whole wheat fettuccine

1 cup packed fresh basil leaves

½ cup pine nuts, toasted*

2 cloves garlic

½ teaspoon salt

¼ teaspoon black pepper

¼ cup plus 1 tablespoon olive oil, divided

Place pine nuts in small saucepan. Heat over low heat 2 minutes or until light brown and fragrant, shaking occasionally.

1. Bring large saucepan of salted water to a boil. Add pasta; cook according to package directions for al dente. Drain; cover to keep warm.

2. Meanwhile, place basil, pine nuts, garlic, salt and pepper in food processor; drizzle with 1 tablespoon olive oil. Process about 10 seconds or until coarsely chopped. With motor running, drizzle in remaining ¼ cup olive oil. Process about 30 seconds or until almost smooth. Toss with hot cooked pasta.

Makes 4 servings

NOTE: Pesto can be made 1 week in advance. Transfer to covered container and store in refrigerator. Makes ½ cup pesto.

LENTIL BOLOGNESE

2 tablespoons olive oil

1 onion, chopped

1 carrot, chopped

1 stalk celery, chopped

2 cloves garlic, minced

1 teaspoon salt

½ teaspoon dried oregano

Pinch red pepper flakes

3 tablespoons tomato paste

¼ cup white wine

1 can (28 ounces) crushed tomatoes

1 can (14 ounces) diced tomatoes

1 cup dried lentils, rinsed

1 portobello mushroom, gills removed, finely chopped

1½ cups water or vegetable broth

12 ounces uncooked whole wheat or regular rotini, cooked according to package directions

1. Heat oil in large saucepan over medium heat. Add onion, carrot and celery; cook and stir 10 minutes or until onion is lightly browned and carrot is softened.

2. Stir in garlic, salt, oregano and red pepper flakes. Add tomato paste; cook and stir 1 minute. Add wine; cook and stir until absorbed. Stir in crushed tomatoes, diced tomatoes, lentils, mushroom and water. Bring to a simmer.

3. Reduce heat to medium; partially cover and simmer about 40 minutes or until lentils are tender, removing cover after 20 minutes. Serve over pasta.

Makes 6 to 8 servings

BOWLS

QUINOA BURRITO BOWLS

1 cup uncooked quinoa

2 cups water

2 tablespoons fresh lime juice, divided

¼ cup vegan sour cream

2 teaspoons vegetable oil

1 small onion, diced

1 red bell pepper, diced

1 clove garlic, minced

½ cup canned black beans, rinsed and drained

½ cup thawed frozen corn

Shredded lettuce

1. Place quinoa in fine-mesh strainer; rinse well under cold running water. Bring 2 cups water to a boil in small saucepan; stir in quinoa. Reduce heat to low; cover and simmer 10 to 15 minutes or until quinoa is tender and water is absorbed. Stir in 1 tablespoon lime juice.

2. Combine sour cream and remaining 1 tablespoon lime juice in small bowl; set aside.

3. Meanwhile, heat oil in large skillet over medium heat. Add onion and bell pepper; cook and stir 5 minutes or until softened. Add garlic; cook 1 minute. Add black beans and corn; cook 3 to 5 minutes or until heated through.

4. Divide quinoa among serving bowls; top with black bean mixture, lettuce and sour cream mixture.

Makes 4 servings

NOTE: This bowl makes a great packable lunch. Layer the quinoa mixture and bean mixture in glass food storage container with lid or glass jar. Pack lettuce and sour cream mixture separately. Heat quinoa and beans in the microwave until warm; top with lettuce and sour cream.

ROASTED CHICKPEA AND SWEET POTATO BOWL

1 sweet potato (about 12 ounces)

1 tablespoon plus 1 teaspoon olive oil, divided

1 teaspoon salt, divided

Black pepper

1 can (15 ounces) chickpeas, rinsed and drained

1 tablespoon maple syrup

1 teaspoon smoked or sweet paprika

½ teaspoon ground cumin

½ cup uncooked quinoa, rinsed

1 cup water

Chopped fresh parsley or cilantro

TAHINI SAUCE

¼ cup tahini

2 tablespoons lemon juice

2 tablespoons water

1 clove garlic, minced

⅛ teaspoon salt

1. Preheat oven to 350°F.

2. Peel sweet potato; cut in half crosswise. Spiral sweet potato with thin ribbon blade of spiralizer. Cut into 3-inch pieces. Place in 13×9-inch pan. Drizzle with 1 teaspoon oil and sprinkle with ¼ teaspoon salt and black pepper; toss to coat. Push to one side of pan.

3. Combine chickpeas, maple syrup, remaining 1 tablespoon oil, paprika, cumin and ½ teaspoon salt in medium bowl; toss to coat. Spread in other side of pan. Bake 30 minutes, stirring potatoes and chickpeas once or twice.

4. Meanwhile, rinse quinoa under cold water in fine-mesh strainer. Bring 1 cup water, quinoa and ¼ teaspoon salt to a boil in small saucepan. Reduce heat to low; cover and simmer 10 to 15 minutes or until quinoa is tender and water is absorbed.

5. For sauce, whisk tahini, lemon juice, 2 tablespoons water, garlic and ⅛ teaspoon salt in small bowl until smooth. Add additional water if needed to reach desired consistency.

6. Divide quinoa between two bowls. Top with sweet potatoes, chickpeas and sauce. Sprinkle with parsley.

Makes 2 servings

NOTE: If you don't have a spiralizer, julienne the sweet potato or cut it into cubes instead.

TOFU SATAY BOWL

1 package (about 12 ounces) extra firm silken tofu, drained*

2 red bell peppers

⅓ cup water

⅓ cup soy sauce

1 tablespoon dark sesame oil

1 teaspoon minced garlic

1 teaspoon minced fresh ginger

24 white or cremini mushrooms, trimmed

Cucumber Relish (recipe follows)

PEANUT SAUCE

1 can (about 13 ounces) coconut milk

½ cup peanut butter

2 tablespoons packed brown sugar

1 tablespoon rice vinegar

2 teaspoons red Thai curry paste

1 cup uncooked jasmine rice, cooked according to package directions

Look for firm and extra firm silken tofu package in aseptic containers in the Asian aisle of the grocery store. If you can't find extra firm silken tofu, use regular firm tofu, drained and pressed.

1. Cut tofu into 24 cubes. Cut each bell pepper into 12 pieces. Combine water, soy sauce, sesame oil, garlic and ginger in large resealable food storage bag. Add tofu, mushrooms and bell pepper. Seal bag; turn to coat. Marinate 30 minutes, turning occasionally. Soak eight 8-inch bamboo skewers in cold water 20 minutes. Meanwhile, prepare cucumber relish.

2. Preheat oven to 400°F. Spray 13×9-inch baking pan with nonstick cooking spray. Drain tofu mixture; discard marinade. Thread tofu and vegetables alternately onto skewers; place in prepared baking pan. Bake 25 minutes or until tofu cubes are lightly browned and vegetables are softened, turning once.

3. Meanwhile, whisk coconut milk, peanut butter, brown sugar, vinegar and curry paste in small saucepan over medium heat. Bring to a boil, stirring constantly. Immediately reduce heat to low. Cook about 20 minutes or until creamy and thick, stirring frequently. Serve tofu, vegetables and sauce over rice with cucumber relish.

Makes 4 servings

CUCUMBER RELISH: Bring ¼ cup rice vinegar, 2 tablespoons sugar and ¼ teaspoon salt to a boil in small saucepan. Pour into large bowl; cool completely. Cut 1 cucumber in half lengthwise; thinly slice. Thinly slice ½ red onion. Peel and julienne 1 carrot. Add vegetables to vinegar mixture. Refrigerate until ready to serve.

RED BEANS AND RICE WITH PICKLED CARROTS AND CUCUMBERS

1 pound dried red kidney beans

1 tablespoon plus 1 teaspoon salt, divided

Pickled Carrots and Cucumbers (recipe follows)

2 tablespoons olive oil

2 onions, chopped

3 stalks celery, chopped

1 green bell pepper, chopped

4 cloves garlic, minced

4 cups vegetable broth

1 teaspoon liquid smoke

1 bay leaf

2 teaspoons Italian seasoning

½ teaspoon black pepper

¼ teaspoon ground red pepper

2 cups uncooked brown rice, cooked according to package directions

Sliced avocado

Hot pepper sauce

1. Place beans in large bowl. Cover with water by at least 2 inches and stir in 1 tablespoon salt. Soak 8 hours or overnight. Meanwhile, prepare pickled carrots and cucumbers.

2. Heat oil in large saucepan over medium-high heat. Add onions; cook and stir 5 minutes. Stir in 1 teaspoon salt. Add celery, bell pepper and garlic; cook and stir 5 minutes or until vegetables are tender.

3. Drain beans; add to saucepan with broth, liquid smoke, bay leaf, Italian seasoning, black pepper and red pepper. Bring to a boil. Reduce heat; simmer, partially covered, 45 minutes.

4. Remove 2 cups bean mixture to medium bowl; let stand 15 minutes to cool slightly. Place in blender or food processor and add ½ cup water; blend until smooth. Stir into beans; continue to cook until beans are tender. Taste and season with additional salt, if desired. Serve in bowls with rice, pickled carrots and cucumbers, avocado and hot pepper sauce.

Makes 6 servings

PICKLED CARROTS AND CUCUMBERS

2 carrots, peeled

1 cucumber

¼ cup water

2 tablespoons sugar

1 tablespoon salt

1 teaspoon peppercorns

2 cloves garlic, smashed

¼ teaspoon dried dill weed

2 bay leaves

1½ cups white vinegar

1. Thinly slice carrots into coins. Very thinly slice cucumber (¹⁄₁₆-inch slices) with a mandoline if you have one. Place carrots and cucumbers in 1-quart jar.

2. Combine water, sugar, salt, peppercorns, garlic, dill and bay leaves in small saucepan. Cook over medium heat just until salt and sugar are dissolved. Pour over vegetables in jar. Add enough vinegar to cover. Seal jar and refrigerate at least 2 hours. Can be made a few days in advance.

DRAGON TOFU

1 package (about 14 ounces) firm tofu, drained

¼ cup soy sauce

1 tablespoon creamy peanut butter

1 medium zucchini

1 medium yellow squash

1 medium red bell pepper

2 teaspoons peanut or vegetable oil

½ teaspoon hot chili oil

2 cloves garlic, minced

2 cups packed torn spinach leaves

¼ cup coarsely chopped cashews or peanuts

1 cup uncooked rice, cooked according to package directions

1. Press tofu lightly between paper towels; cut into ¾-inch squares or triangles. Place in single layer in shallow dish. Whisk soy sauce into peanut butter in small bowl until smooth. Pour mixture over tofu; stir gently to coat. Let stand at room temperature 20 minutes.

2. Meanwhile, cut zucchini and yellow squash lengthwise into ¼-inch-thick slices; cut each slice into 2-inch strips. Cut bell pepper into 2-inch strips.

3. Heat peanut oil and chili oil in large skillet over medium-high heat. Add garlic, zucchini, yellow squash and bell pepper; stir-fry 3 minutes. Add tofu mixture; cook 2 minutes or until tofu is heated through and sauce is slightly thickened, stirring occasionally. Stir in spinach; remove from heat. Sprinkle with cashews. Stir in bowls with rice.

Makes 2 servings

MUJADARA

- 1 cup brown lentils, rinsed and sorted
- 3 sweet onions, thinly sliced
- ¼ cup plus 1 tablespoon olive oil, divided
- 2½ teaspoons salt, divided
- 1½ teaspoons ground cumin
- 1 teaspoon ground allspice
- 1 cinnamon stick
- 1 bay leaf
- ⅛ to ¼ teaspoon ground red pepper
- ¾ cup uncooked long grain white rice, rinsed and drained
- 3 cups vegetable broth or water
- 1 cucumber
- 1 cup vegan sour cream

1. Place lentils in medium saucepan; cover with water by 1 inch. Bring to a boil over medium-high heat. Reduce heat to medium-low; simmer 10 minutes. Drain and rinse under cold water.

2. Meanwhile, heat ¼ cup oil in large saucepan or Dutch oven. Add onions and 1 teaspoon salt; cook and stir 15 minutes or until golden and parts are crispy. Remove most of onions to small bowl, leaving about ½ cup in saucepan.*

3. Add remaining 1 tablespoon oil to saucepan with onions; heat over medium-high heat. Add cumin, allspice, cinnamon stick, bay leaf and red pepper; cook and stir 30 seconds. Add rice; cook and stir 2 to 3 minutes or until rice is lightly toasted. Add broth, lentils and 1 teaspoon salt; bring to a boil. Reduce heat to low; cover and cook about 15 minutes or until broth is absorbed and rice and lentils are tender. Remove saucepan from heat. Place clean kitchen towel over top of saucepan; replace lid and let stand 5 to 10 minutes.

4. Meanwhile, peel cucumber and trim ends. Grate cucumber on large holes of box grater; squeeze out excess liquid. Place in medium bowl; stir in sour cream and remaining ½ teaspoon salt. Serve lentils and rice with reserved onions and cucumber sauce.

If desired, continue to cook reserved onions in a medium skillet over medium heat until dark golden brown.

Makes 4 to 6 servings

PICANTE PINTOS AND RICE

2 cups dried pinto beans, rinsed and sorted

2 cups water

1 can (about 14 ounces) stewed tomatoes

1 cup coarsely chopped onion

¾ cup coarsely chopped green bell pepper

¼ cup sliced celery

4 cloves garlic, minced

½ small jalapeño pepper, seeded and chopped

2 teaspoons dried oregano

2 teaspoons chili powder

1 teaspoon salt

½ teaspoon ground red pepper

2 cups chopped kale

1 cup uncooked brown rice, cooked according to package directions

1. Place beans in large saucepan; add water to cover beans by 2 inches. Bring to a boil over high heat; boil 2 minutes. Remove from heat; let stand, covered, 1 hour. Drain beans; discard water. Return beans to saucepan.

2. Add 2 cups water, tomatoes, onion, bell pepper, celery, garlic, jalapeño, oregano, chili powder, salt and red pepper to saucepan; bring to a boil over high heat. Reduce heat to low. Simmer, covered, about 1½ hours or until beans are tender, stirring occasionally.

3. Gently stir kale into bean mixture. Simmer, uncovered, 30 minutes. (Beans will be very tender.) Serve in bowls over rice.

Makes 4 to 6 servings

ROASTED VEGETABLE RAMEN BOWL

3 tablespoons soy sauce, divided

3 tablespoons peanut or vegetable oil

2 tablespoons rice vinegar

2 cloves garlic, minced

8 ounces sliced mushrooms

1 medium zucchini, cut in half lengthwise then crosswise into 1-inch pieces

1 medium yellow squash, cut in half lengthwise then crosswise into 1-inch pieces

1 red bell pepper, cut into 1-inch pieces

1 yellow bell pepper, cut into 1-inch pieces

2 cups cubed eggplant

3 shallots

2 packages (3 ounces each) ramen noodles, any flavor* *or* 6 ounces spaghetti

1 tablespoon dark sesame oil

Chopped fresh basil or parsley (optional)

Discard seasoning packets.

1. Preheat oven to 425°F. Combine 2 tablespoons soy sauce, peanut oil, vinegar and garlic in small bowl.

2. Spray sheet pan with nonstick cooking spray. Combine mushrooms, zucchini, yellow squash, bell peppers, eggplant and shallots in prepared pan. Drizzle with soy sauce mixture; toss to coat.

3. Roast 20 minutes or until browned and tender, stirring well after 10 minutes.

4. Prepare noodles according to package directions. Drain and place in large bowl. Toss noodles with remaining 1 tablespoon soy sauce and sesame oil.

5. Divide noodles among bowls; top with vegetables and basil.

Makes 4 to 6 servings

FARRO, GRAPE AND ROASTED CARROT BOWL

1 pound carrots, peeled, trimmed and halved lengthwise

¼ cup olive oil, divided

1 teaspoon salt, divided

½ teaspoon ground cumin

¼ teaspoon ground coriander

⅛ teaspoon ground nutmeg

1 package (2¼ ounces) slivered almonds

2 cups water

1 cup uncooked farro, rinsed under cold water

2 tablespoons balsamic vinegar

1 cup halved red grapes

¼ cup minced red onion

Salt and black pepper

4 cups mixed spring greens

1. Preheat oven to 375°F. Place carrots on sheet pan. Drizzle with 1 tablespoon oil. Combine ½ teaspoon salt, cumin, coriander and nutmeg in small bowl; sprinkle over carrots. Toss to coat carrots with oil and spices. Arrange cut sides down in single layer.

2. Roast 30 minutes or until carrots are browned and tender, turning once. Place almonds on small baking sheet; bake about 5 minutes or until almonds are toasted, stirring frequently.

3. Meanwhile, bring 2 cups water and remaining ½ teaspoon salt to a boil in medium saucepan. Stir in farro; reduce heat to medium-low. Cover and simmer 25 minutes or until tender. Drain and place farro in large bowl.

4. Whisk remaining 3 tablespoons oil into vinegar in small bowl; pour over farro. Stir in grapes and onion; season to taste with additional salt and pepper. Cut carrots into 1-inch pieces; add to farro mixture. Place greens in bowls; top with farro salad and sprinkle with almonds.

Makes 4 to 6 servings

CHICKPEA TIKKA MASALA

1 tablespoon olive oil

1 onion, chopped

3 cloves garlic, minced

1 tablespoon minced fresh ginger or ginger paste

1 tablespoon garam masala

1 teaspoon ground cumin

1 teaspoon ground coriander

1 teaspoon salt

¼ teaspoon ground red pepper

2 cans (15 ounces each) chickpeas, drained

1 can (28 ounces) crushed tomatoes

1 can (about 13 ounces) coconut milk

1 package (about 12 ounces) firm silken tofu, drained and cut into 1-inch cubes

1 cup uncooked brown basmati rice, cooked according to package directions

Chopped fresh cilantro

1. Heat oil in large saucepan over medium-high heat. Add onion; cook and stir 5 minutes or until translucent. Add garlic, ginger, garam masala, cumin, coriander, salt and red pepper; cook and stir 1 minute.

2. Stir in chickpeas, tomatoes and coconut milk; simmer 30 minutes or until thickened and chickpeas have softened slightly. Add tofu; stir gently. Cook 7 to 10 minutes or until tofu is heated through. Serve in bowls with rice; garnish with cilantro.

Makes 4 servings

PEANUT BUTTER TOFU BOWL

SAUCE

- ¼ cup peanut butter
- ¼ cup hoisin sauce
- 1 tablespoon packed brown sugar
- 1 tablespoon dark sesame oil
- 1 tablespoon water
- 1½ teaspoons minced fresh ginger
- 1½ teaspoons unseasoned rice vinegar
- 1½ teaspoons soy sauce
- 1 clove garlic, minced
- ½ teaspoon sriracha sauce

BOWL

- 1 package (about 14 ounces) firm tofu, pressed, cut into 24 (1-inch) cubes
- ¼ cup cornstarch
- 2 tablespoons plus 1 teaspoon vegetable oil, divided
- 1 head bok choy
- 1 clove garlic, minced
- 1 tablespoon soy sauce
- 1 tablespoon rice vinegar
- 1 cup uncooked rice, cooked according to package directions
- Chopped peanuts (optional)

1. For sauce, combine peanut butter, hoisin, brown sugar, sesame oil, 1 tablespoon water, ginger, 1½ teaspoons vinegar, 1½ teaspoons soy sauce, 1 clove garlic and sriracha in small saucepan. Cook over medium-low heat 5 minutes, whisking frequently.

2. Toss tofu with cornstarch in large bowl. Heat 2 tablespoons vegetable oil in large nonstick skillet over high heat. Add tofu to skillet; cook without stirring 5 minutes or until well browned and crusted on bottom. Turn and cook 5 minutes or until browned on other side. Cook 2 minutes, turning frequently until other sides of tofu are lightly browned. Add sauce; cook 1 minute or until tofu is glazed.

3. Meanwhile, separate leaves and stems of bok choy. Coarsely chop stems and leaves separately. Heat remaining 1 teaspoon vegetable oil in medium skillet over medium-high heat. Add bok choy stems; cook and stir 3 minutes. Add leaves and 1 clove garlic; cook and stir 1 minute. Add 1 tablespoon soy sauce and 1 tablespoon vinegar; cook and stir 30 seconds.

4. Divide tofu, bok choy and rice among bowls. Garnish with peanuts.

Makes 4 servings

SESAME NOODLE BOWL

1 package (16 ounces) uncooked spaghetti

6 tablespoons soy sauce

5 tablespoons dark sesame oil

3 tablespoons sugar

3 tablespoons rice vinegar

4 tablespoons vegetable oil, divided

3 cloves garlic, minced

1 teaspoon grated fresh ginger or ginger paste

½ teaspoon sriracha sauce

2 green onions, sliced

1 red bell pepper, cut into thin strips

1 cucumber

1 carrot

1 package (about 14 ounces) firm tofu, drained and patted dry

Sesame seeds (optional)

1. Cook spaghetti according to package directions until al dente in large saucepan of boiling salted water. Drain, reserving 1 tablespoon pasta cooking water.

2. Whisk soy sauce, sesame oil, sugar, vinegar, 2 tablespoons vegetable oil, garlic, ginger and sriracha in large bowl. Stir in noodles, reserved pasta cooking water and green onions. Let stand at least 30 minutes until noodles have cooled to room temperature and most of sauce is absorbed, stirring occasionally.

3. Meanwhile, cut bell pepper into thin strips. Peel cucumber and carrot and shred with julienne peeler into long strands, or cut into thin strips.

4. Cut tofu into thin triangles or 1-inch cubes. Heat remaining 2 tablespoons oil in large nonstick skillet over high heat. Add tofu; cook 5 minutes or until browned on all sides, turning occasionally.

5. Place noodles in bowls. Top with tofu, bell pepper, cucumber and carrot. Sprinkle with sesame seeds, if desired.

Makes 6 servings

NOTE: Sesame noodles are great served warm or cold. To serve them cold, cover and refrigerate a few hours or overnight after step 2 before preparing the vegetables and tofu. For a side dish or potluck dish, skip the tofu and stir the vegetables into the noodles after they are cool. Refrigerate until ready to serve.

KOSHARI

5 cups water

3 teaspoons kosher salt, divided

1 cup dried lentils, rinsed and sorted

1 cup uncooked white basmati rice, rinsed and drained

1 teaspoon ground cinnamon, divided

½ teaspoon ground nutmeg, divided

1 cup uncooked elbow macaroni

¼ cup olive oil

1 large onion, thinly sliced

1 large onion, diced

1 tablespoon minced garlic

1 teaspoon ground cumin

½ teaspoon ground coriander

¼ teaspoon red pepper flakes

¼ teaspoon black pepper

1 can (28 ounces) crushed tomatoes

2 teaspoons red wine vinegar

1. Bring water and 2 teaspoons salt to a boil in large saucepan. Stir in lentils, rice, ½ teaspoon cinnamon and ¼ teaspoon nutmeg; reduce heat to medium. Simmer, partially covered, 7 minutes. Stir in macaroni; cover and cook 8 minutes or until lentils, rice and macaroni are tender. Remove from heat. Place clean kitchen towel over top of pot. Cover with lid and let stand 10 minutes.

2. Meanwhile, heat oil in large skillet over medium-high heat. Add sliced onion; cook 12 minutes or until edges are dark brown and onion is softened. Transfer onions to medium bowl using tongs or slotted spoon, leaving oil in skillet. Season with ¼ teaspoon salt. Set aside.

3. Heat same skillet with oil over medium heat. Add diced onion; cook 8 minutes or until softened. Add garlic, cumin, coriander, remaining ½ teaspoon cinnamon, red pepper flakes, black pepper and remaining ¼ teaspoon nutmeg; cook 30 seconds or until fragrant. Stir in tomatoes, vinegar and remaining ¾ teaspoon salt; cook 8 to 10 minutes or until thickened, stirring occasionally.

4. Fluff rice mixture with fork. Place in bowls; top with sauce and fried onions.

Makes 6 to 8 servings

DESSERTS

PINEAPPLE UPSIDE DOWN CAKE

TOPPING

- ½ **cup packed brown sugar**
- ¼ **cup vegan buttery spread**
- 7 **canned or fresh pineapple slices**
- 7 **maraschino cherries**

CAKE

- 3 **tablespoons boiling water**
- 1 **tablespoon ground flaxseed**
- 2 **cups all-purpose flour**
- 2 **teaspoons baking powder**
- ½ **teaspoon salt**
- 1 **cup granulated sugar**
- ½ **cup vegetable oil**
- 1 **teaspoon vanilla**
- 1 **cup refrigerated coconut milk beverage**
- ½ **teaspoon baking soda**
- 1 **tablespoon apple cider vinegar**

1. Preheat oven to 350°F. Grease 9-inch round baking pan.

2. For topping, cook and stir brown sugar and buttery spread in medium skillet over medium heat until melted and smooth. Remove from heat. Pour into prepared pan. Arrange pineapple slices in pan, placing cherries in centers of pineapple.

3. Combine boiling water and flaxseed in small bowl. Let stand until cool. Whisk flour, baking powder and salt in medium bowl. Whisk granulated sugar, oil and vanilla in large bowl until well blended. Whisk in flaxseed mixture. Stir in flour mixture just until moistened. Stir in coconut milk just until blended. Place baking soda in small cup; stir in vinegar. Gently stir vinegar mixture into batter just until blended. Pour batter over pineapple.

4. Bake 45 to 50 minutes or until toothpick inserted into center comes out clean. Cool in pan on wire rack 10 minutes. Run thin knife around edge of pan to loosen cake. Invert onto serving plate. Cool completely.

Makes 10 servings

NOTE: The cake can also be baked in a 12-inch cast iron skillet. Melt the buttery spread and brown sugar in the skillet, add the pineapple and cherries and pour the batter over the fruit. Check the cake for doneness at 40 minutes.

COCONUT MILK ICE CREAM

2 cans (about 13 ounces each) unsweetened coconut milk

½ cup sugar

4 ounces vegan bittersweet chocolate, finely chopped

1. Combine coconut milk and sugar in medium saucepan. Cook over medium-low heat, whisking constantly, until smooth and sugar is dissolved. Refrigerate until cold.

2. Process in ice cream maker according to manufacturer's directions, adding chocolate during last 2 minutes. Transfer to freezer container and freeze until firm.

3. To serve, let ice cream soften slightly at room temperature, or microwave 20 to 30 seconds on HIGH.

Makes about 1 quart

NOTE: For fine chocolate pieces in your ice cream, melt the chocolate and let it cool. Pour it into the ice cream maker in thin steady stream and process just until the chocolate is evenly distributed through the ice cream.

CHOCOLATE-ALMOND CRISPY TREATS

6 cups crisp brown rice cereal

1½ cups sliced almonds, toasted*

1 cup light corn syrup

⅓ cup almond butter or peanut butter

¼ cup packed brown sugar

3 tablespoons unsweetened cocoa powder

¼ teaspoon salt

1 cup vegan semisweet chocolate chips

*To toast almonds, spread in single layer in heavy skillet. Cook over medium heat 1 to 2 minutes or until nuts are lightly browned, stirring frequently.

1. Line 13×9-inch baking pan with parchment paper. Spray with nonstick cooking spray.

2. Combine rice cereal and almonds in large bowl; set aside.

3. Combine corn syrup, almond butter, brown sugar, cocoa and salt in large saucepan. Cook and stir over medium heat 5 minutes or until mixture is smooth and just begins to boil across surface. Remove from heat.

4. Immediately stir cereal mixture into saucepan. Gently fold in chocolate chips. Press firmly into prepared pan. Let stand 1 hour or until set. Cut into bars.

Makes 24 bars

EASY ORANGE CAKE

1½ cups all-purpose flour

1 cup sugar

Grated peel of 1 orange

1 teaspoon baking soda

¼ teaspoon salt

1 cup orange juice

5 tablespoons vegetable oil

Orange No-Butter Buttercream Frosting (recipe follows)

Candied orange peel (optional)

1. Preheat oven to 350°F. Spray 9-inch round cake pan with nonstick cooking spray.

2. Combine flour, sugar, orange peel, baking soda and salt in medium bowl. Combine orange juice and oil in small bowl or measuring cup. Add to flour mixture; stir until smooth. Spread batter in prepared pan.

3. Bake 30 minutes or until toothpick inserted into center comes out clean. Cool cake in pan 10 minutes. Remove to wire rack; cool completely.

4. Meanwhile, prepare frosting. Frost cake; garnish with candied orange peel.

Makes about 6 servings

ORANGE NO-BUTTER BUTTERCREAM FROSTING

½ cup (1 stick) vegan buttery spread, softened

2 teaspoons grated orange peel

2 tablespoons orange juice

1 teaspoon vanilla

4 cups powdered sugar

4 to 6 tablespoons soy creamer

1. Beat spread in medium bowl with electric mixer at medium speed until light and fluffy. Beat in orange peel, orange juice and vanilla.

2. Gradually beat in powdered sugar. Beat in soy creamer by tablespoonfuls until spreading consistency is reached.

CARROT GINGER CUPCAKES

3 cups all-purpose flour

⅓ cup coarsely chopped pecans, plus additional for garnish

2 teaspoons baking powder

1 teaspoon baking soda

1 teaspoon salt

½ teaspoon ground cinnamon

¾ cup water

3 tablespoons ground flaxseed

1½ cups granulated sugar

½ cup vegetable oil

½ cup (1 stick) vegan buttery spread, softened

1 tablespoon vanilla

1 pound carrots, shredded

Grated peel of 2 oranges

Juice of 1 orange

2 tablespoons grated fresh ginger

FROSTING

½ cup (1 stick) vegan buttery spread, softened

4½ cups powdered sugar

¼ cup orange juice

1 tablespoon grated fresh ginger

1 teaspoon vanilla

1. Preheat oven to 350°F. Line 24 standard (2½-inch) muffin cups with paper baking cups.

2. Whisk flour, ⅓ cup pecans, baking powder, baking soda, salt and cinnamon in medium bowl. Combine water and flaxseed in small saucepan; bring to a boil over medium-high heat. Reduce heat to low; simmer 3 minutes. Cool to room temperature.

3. Beat granulated sugar, oil and ½ cup spread in large bowl with electric mixer at medium speed until light and fluffy. Beat in flaxseed mixture and 1 tablespoon vanilla. Add carrots, orange peel, juice of one orange and 2 tablespoons ginger; mix well. Add flour mixture; mix just until combined. Spoon batter evenly into prepared muffin cups.

4. Bake 22 to 25 minutes or until toothpick inserted into centers comes out clean. Cool in pans 10 minutes. Remove to wire racks; cool completely.

5. For frosting, beat ½ cup spread in large bowl with electric mixer at medium speed until creamy. Gradually add powdered sugar, beating well after each addition. Beat in ¼ cup orange juice, 1 tablespoon ginger and 1 teaspoon vanilla; beat at medium-high speed at least 1 minute or until well blended and fluffy.

6. Frost cupcakes; sprinkle with additional chopped pecans. Refrigerate until ready to serve.

MIXED BERRY CRISP

6 cups mixed berries, thawed if frozen

¾ cup packed brown sugar, divided

¼ cup quick-cooking tapioca

Juice of ½ lemon

1 teaspoon ground cinnamon

½ cup rice flour

6 tablespoons cold vegan buttery spread, cut into small pieces

½ cup sliced almonds

1. Preheat oven to 375°F. Spray 8- or 9-inch square baking dish with nonstick cooking spray.

2. Combine berries, ¼ cup brown sugar, tapioca, lemon juice and cinnamon in large bowl; toss to coat. Spoon into prepared baking dish.

3. Combine rice flour, remaining ½ cup brown sugar and spread in food processor; pulse until mixture resembles coarse crumbs. Add almonds; pulse until combined. (Leave some large pieces of almonds.) Sprinkle over berry mixture.

4. Bake 20 to 30 minutes or until topping is golden brown.

Makes about 9 servings

APPLE CAKE

4 medium apples, peeled and cut into ¼-inch slices (4 cups)

Juice of ½ lemon

1 cup plus 1 tablespoon sugar, divided

3 cups all-purpose flour

¾ cup chopped almonds

1½ teaspoons baking soda

1 teaspoon ground cinnamon

½ teaspoon salt

½ teaspoon ground nutmeg

1 cup vegetable oil

1 teaspoon vanilla

1. Preheat oven to 350°F. Spray 13×9-inch baking pan with nonstick cooking spray.

2. Place apples in medium bowl. Drizzle with lemon juice and sprinkle with 1 tablespoon sugar; toss to coat. Let stand 20 minutes or until juice forms.

3. Combine flour, remaining 1 cup sugar, almonds, baking soda, cinnamon, salt and nutmeg in large bowl; mix well. Add oil and vanilla; stir until well blended. Stir in apple mixture. Spread batter in prepared pan.

4. Bake about 35 minutes or until browned and toothpick inserted into center comes out clean. Cool in pan on wire rack 10 minutes. Serve warm.

Makes 16 servings

NOTE: Either whole skin-on almonds or sliced almonds can be used.

COCONUT, PEANUT BUTTER AND QUINOA TRUFFLES

½ cup uncooked quinoa

1 cup water

2 cups sweetened flaked coconut (about ½ of 14-ounce package), divided

½ cup creamy peanut butter

2 tablespoons maple syrup

½ teaspoon ground cinnamon

½ teaspoon vanilla

1. Place quinoa in fine-mesh strainer; rinse well under cold water. Combine 1 cup water and quinoa in medium saucepan; bring to a boil over high heat. Reduce heat to low; cover and simmer 10 to 15 minutes or until quinoa is tender and water is absorbed. Cool slightly.

2. Meanwhile, spread coconut in medium skillet. Cook and stir over medium heat until lightly brown and toasted, stirring frequently. Cool slightly.

3. Combine quinoa, 1¼ cups coconut, peanut butter, maple syrup, cinnamon and vanilla in medium bowl.

4. Shape mixture into 1-inch balls. Roll in remaining ¾ cup coconut to coat. Store leftovers in refrigerator.

Makes 24 servings

TRIPLE GINGER COOKIES

3 tablespoons boiling water

1 tablespoon ground flaxseed

2 cups all-purpose flour

2 teaspoons baking soda

1 teaspoon ground ginger

½ teaspoon salt

¾ cup (1½ sticks) vegan buttery spread

1¼ cups sugar, divided

¼ cup molasses

1 tablespoon grated fresh ginger

1 tablespoon finely minced crystallized ginger*

Semisoft sugar-coated ginger slices are preferable to the small dry ginger cubes found on supermarket spice shelves. The softer, larger slices are available at natural foods or specialty stores. If using the small dry cubes of ginger, steep the cubes in boiling water a few minutes to soften, then drain, pat dry and mince.

1. Combine boiling water and flaxseed in small bowl. Let stand until cool. Whisk flour, baking soda, ground ginger and salt in medium bowl until well blended.

2. Melt spread in small heavy saucepan over low heat; pour into large bowl and cool slightly. Add 1 cup sugar, molasses and flaxseed mixture; mix well. Add flour mixture; mix well. Add fresh ginger and crystallized ginger; mix just until blended. Cover and refrigerate 1 hour.

3. Preheat oven to 375°F. Line cookie sheets with parchment paper. Roll dough into 1-inch balls. Place remaining ¼ cup sugar in shallow dish; roll balls of dough in sugar to coat. Place 3 inches apart on prepared cookie sheets. (If dough is very sticky, drop by teaspoonfuls into sugar to coat.)

4. For chewy cookies, bake 7 minutes or until edges just start to brown. For crisper cookies, bake 9 to 11 minutes. Cool on cookie sheets 1 minute. Remove to wire racks; cool completely.

Makes 3 dozen cookies

VARIATION: Roll dough in plastic wrap to form a log. Refrigerate up to 1 week or freeze up to 2 months. To bake, bring the dough nearly to room temperature and slice. Dip the tops in sugar and bake as directed.

DOUBLE CHOCOLATE COOKIES AND CREAM MOUSSE

4 ounces vegan semisweet chocolate, chopped

½ cup aquafaba* from 1 (15-ounce) can of chickpeas

1 teaspoon vanilla

¼ teaspoon salt

¼ teaspoon cream of tartar

½ cup sugar

Chopped vegan chocolate sandwich cookies

Vegan whipped topping (optional)

Liquid from cans of chickpeas.

1. Melt chocolate in medium saucepan over very low heat, stirring frequently. Remove from heat; cool completely.

2. Combine aquafaba, vanilla, salt and cream of tartar in bowl of electric mixer. Attach whisk attachment to mixer. Whip on high speed 5 minutes or until soft peaks form. Gradually add sugar 1 tablespoon at a time; beat 5 minutes or until thick and glossy and stiff peaks form. Add melted chocolate; whip until well blended. Scrape bottom and side of bowl; whip until mixture deflates slightly to consistency of pudding.

3. Layer mousse and chopped sandwich cookies in 4 to 6 jars or small serving bowls; refrigerate at least 1 hour or until cold and set. Pipe or dollop whipped topping onto each serving, if desired. Top with additional chopped cookies.

Makes 4 to 6 servings

GLAZED APPLESAUCE SPICE CAKE

½ cup boiling water

3 tablespoons ground flaxseed

2¼ cups all-purpose flour

2 teaspoons baking soda

2 teaspoons ground cinnamon

½ teaspoon ground nutmeg

½ teaspoon ground ginger

½ teaspoon salt

1 cup packed brown sugar

¾ cup coconut oil or vegan buttery spread

1½ teaspoons vanilla

1½ cups unsweetened applesauce

½ cup plain unsweetened soymilk

⅔ cup chopped walnuts

1 cup powdered sugar

2 tablespoons apple cider or apple juice concentrate

1. Preheat oven to 350°F. Grease and flour 12-cup bundt pan or 10-inch tube pan. Combine boiling water and flaxseed in small bowl. Let stand until cool. Combine flour, baking soda, cinnamon, nutmeg, ginger and salt in medium bowl.

2. Beat brown sugar and coconut oil in large bowl with electric mixer on medium speed until blended. Beat in flaxseed mixture and vanilla until well blended. Add flour mixture alternately with applesauce and soymilk, beginning and ending with flour mixture, beating well after each addition. Stir in walnuts. Pour into prepared pan.

3. Bake 50 to 55 minutes or until toothpick inserted near center comes out clean. Cool in pan 15 minutes. Loosen from pan; invert onto wire rack to cool completely.

4. Combine powdered sugar and apple cider in small bowl; whisk until smooth. Spoon glaze over top of cake. Store tightly covered at room temperature.

Makes 12 servings

BLUEBERRY LEMON CORNMEAL COBBLER

3 tablespoons boiling water

1 tablespoon ground flaxseed

5 cups fresh blueberries

½ cup plus ⅓ cup sugar, divided

3 tablespoons lemon juice, divided

2 tablespoons cornstarch

1½ tablespoons finely grated lemon peel, divided

½ cup plain unsweetened soymilk or almond milk

¾ cup all-purpose flour

¼ cup fine-ground cornmeal

1½ teaspoons baking powder

¼ teaspoon salt

¼ cup coconut oil, melted

1. Preheat oven to 375°F. Spray 8-inch square baking pan with nonstick cooking spray. Combine boiling water and flaxseed in small bowl. Let stand until cool.

2. Combine blueberries, ⅓ cup sugar, 1 tablespoon lemon juice, cornstarch and ½ tablespoon lemon peel in large bowl; toss to coat. Spoon into prepared pan.

3. Combine soymilk and remaining 2 tablespoons lemon juice in small bowl; let stand 5 minutes. Combine flour, cornmeal, remaining ½ cup sugar, 1 tablespoon lemon peel, baking powder and salt in medium bowl; mix well. Add soymilk mixture, coconut oil and flaxseed mixture; stir just until combined. Drop topping by 2 tablespoons into mounds over blueberry mixture.

4. Bake 40 to 45 minutes or until filling is bubbly and topping is golden brown. Let stand 30 minutes before serving.

Makes 8 to 10 servings

CHAI BROWN RICE PUDDING

4 English breakfast tea bags

4 cups plain unsweetened soymilk or almond milk

½ cup uncooked short grain brown rice, rinsed well

¼ cup chia seeds

2 tablespoons packed brown sugar

2 tablespoons agave nectar

1 teaspoon ground cinnamon

½ teaspoon ground ginger

¼ teaspoon salt

¼ teaspoon ground cardamom

¼ cup raisins

Vegan whipped topping (optional)

1. Pour 1 cup boiling water over tea bags in liquid measuring cup. Steep 5 minutes; discard tea bags.

2. Combine tea, soymilk, rice, chia seeds, brown sugar, agave, cinnamon, ginger, salt and cardamom in large saucepan. Bring to a boil over medium-high heat. Reduce heat to low.

3. Cook, partially covered, 1½ hours until rice is tender and mixture is thick and creamy, stirring occasionally. Skim off any film that appears on surface. Stir in raisins.

4. Serve warm or at room temperature. Top with whipped topping, if desired.

Makes 4 servings

CHOCOLATE CAKE

CAKE

- 6 tablespoons boiling water
- 2 tablespoons ground flaxseed
- 2 cups granulated sugar
- 2 cups all-purpose flour
- 1 cup unsweetened cocoa powder
- 1 tablespoon instant espresso powder*
- 1½ teaspoons baking soda
- 1½ teaspoons baking powder
- 1½ teaspoons salt
- ¾ cup plain unsweetened almond milk
- ½ cup vegetable oil
- 1 tablespoon apple cider vinegar
- 2 teaspoons vanilla
- 1 cup hot water*

FROSTING

- 1 package (12 ounces) vegan chocolate chips
- ¼ teaspoon salt
- 1 can (about 13 ounces) full-fat coconut milk
- 2 cups powdered sugar
- Multicolored vegan decors (optional)

Or substitute 1 cup hot strong coffee for the espresso powder and hot water.

1. Preheat oven to 350°F. Line 13×9-inch baking pan with parchment paper or spray with nonstick cooking spray. Combine boiling water and flaxseed in small bowl; cool completely.

2. Whisk granulated sugar, flour, cocoa, espresso powder, baking soda, baking powder and 1½ teaspoons salt in large bowl. Make well in center. Pour almond milk, oil, vinegar, vanilla and flaxseed mixture into well; whisk gently to blend wet ingredients. Whisk into dry ingredients until moistened. Add hot water; whisk until well blended. Pour into prepared pan.

3. Bake about 35 minutes or until top appears dry and toothpick inserted into center comes out clean. Cool completely in pan on wire rack.

4. For frosting, place chocolate chips and ¼ teaspoon salt in bowl of electric mixer. Bring coconut milk to a simmer in small saucepan over medium heat, whisking frequently to blend. Pour 1 cup coconut milk over chips; swirl to coat. Let stand 5 minutes; whisk until smooth. Cool to room temperature.** Add powdered sugar; beat on low speed until blended. Increase speed to medium-high; beat 1 to 2 minutes or until frosting is fluffy and smooth. If frosting is too thick, add remaining coconut milk by teaspoonfuls until desired consistency is reached. Spread frosting over cake; sprinkle with decors, if desired.

**To frost cake with ganache instead of frosting, spread cooled mixture over top of cake (skip the powdered sugar). For firm ganache, refrigerate until set.

Makes 12 to 16 servings

PLUM RHUBARB CRUMBLE

1½ pounds plums, each pitted and cut into 8 wedges (4 cups)

1½ pounds rhubarb, cut into ½-inch pieces (5 cups)

1 cup granulated sugar

1 teaspoon finely grated fresh ginger

¼ teaspoon ground nutmeg

3 tablespoons cornstarch

¾ cup old-fashioned oats

½ cup all-purpose flour

½ cup packed brown sugar

½ cup sliced almonds, toasted*

¼ teaspoon salt

½ cup coconut oil

*To toast almonds, spread in single layer in heavy skillet. Cook over medium heat 1 to 2 minutes or until nuts are lightly browned, stirring frequently.

1. Combine plums, rhubarb, granulated sugar, ginger and nutmeg in large bowl; toss to coat. Cover and let stand at room temperature 2 hours.

2. Preheat oven to 375°F. Spray 9-inch round or square baking dish with nonstick cooking spray. Line baking sheet with foil.

3. Pour juices from fruit mixture into small saucepan; bring to a boil over medium-high heat. Cook about 12 minutes or until reduced to syrupy consistency, stirring occasionally. Stir in cornstarch until well blended. Stir mixture into bowl with fruit; pour into prepared baking dish.

4. Combine oats, flour, brown sugar, almonds and salt in medium bowl; mix well. Add coconut oil; mix with fingertips until butter is evenly distributed and mixture is clumpy. Sprinkle evenly over fruit mixture. Place baking dish on prepared baking sheet.

5. Bake about 50 minutes or until filling is bubbly and topping is golden brown. Cool 1 hour before serving.

Makes 6 to 8 servings

CHOCOLATE CHIP COOKIES

2 cups all-purpose flour

1 teaspoon baking soda

½ teaspoon salt

¼ teaspoon baking powder

¾ cup coconut oil, melted and cooled slightly

¾ cup packed brown sugar

½ cup granulated sugar

½ cup water

1¼ teaspoons vanilla

1 package (12 ounces) vegan semisweet chocolate chips

Flaky sea salt (optional)

1. Whisk flour, baking soda, ½ teaspoon salt and ¼ teaspoon baking powder in medium bowl.

2. Whisk coconut oil, sugars, water and vanilla in large bowl until well blended. Add flour mixture; stir until well blended. Add chocolate chips; mix well. Cover and refrigerate at least 1 hour or until firm.

3. Preheat oven to 350°F. Line baking sheets with parchment paper. For each cookie, shape about 2 tablespoons of dough into 1½-inch ball; place 9 balls on each prepared baking sheet. Sprinkle with sea salt, if desired.

4. Bake about 12 minutes or until centers are set and edges are lightly browned. Cool cookies on baking sheets 5 minutes. Remove to wire racks; cool completely.

Makes about 18 cookies

NOTE: These cookies are great the day they're made but the flavor and texture are even better the next day.

INDEX

A

Apple Cake, 230

Apples
  Apple Cake, 230
  Cucumber Basil Cooler, 36
  Melonade, 35
  Orchard Crush Juice, 32
  Roasted Sweet Potato and
    Apple Salad, 100
  Sharp Apple Cooler, 34
  Tangerapple Juice, 33
  Wheat Berry Apple Salad, 84

Artichokes: Spinach-Artichoke
  Lasagna, 168

Avocado
  Avocado Toast, 17
  Chopped Salad with
    Cornbread Croutons, 106
  Persimmon and Chickpea
    Salad, 110
  Spinach Veggie Wrap, 152
  Tortilla Cups with Corn and
    Black Bean Salsa, 56
Avocado Toast, 17

B

Balsamic Butternut Squash, 94

Bananas: Peanut Butter Banana
  Blend, 37
Barbecue Seitan Skewers, 70

Barley
  Barley with Currants and Pine
    Nuts, 86
  Fruity Whole-Grain Cereal, 30
  Garden Vegetable Soup, 116
Barley with Currants and Pine
  Nuts, 86

Beans
  Beans and Greens Crostini,
    44
  Black Bean Sliders, 52
  Black Bean Soup, 115
  Cauliflower Tacos with
    Chipotle Crema, 146

Beans *(continued)*
  Cold Peanut Noodles with
    Edamame, 172
  Four-Bean Chili, 126
  Jamaican Black Bean Stew,
    118
  Minestrone Soup, 124
  Picante Pintos and Rice, 204
  Quinoa and Roasted Corn,
    102
  Quinoa Burrito Bowls, 193
  Rainbow Vegetable Stew, 130
  Red Beans and Rice with
    Pickled Carrots and
    Cucumbers,
    198
  Ribollita (Tuscan Bread Soup),
    136
  Texas Caviar, 76
  Tortilla Cups with Corn and
    Black Bean Salsa, 56
  White Beans and Tomatoes,
    120
Beans and Greens Crostini, 44

Berries
  Berry Soy-Cream Blend, 34
  Blueberry Lemon Cornmeal
    Cobbler, 240
  Mixed Berry Crisp, 228
  Orchard Crush Juice, 32
Berry Soy-Cream Blend, 34
Black Bean Sliders, 52
Black Bean Soup, 115
Blueberry Lemon Cornmeal
  Cobbler, 240

Breads
  Cornbread, 107
  Pita Bread, 64
  Scallion Pancakes, 62
  Socca (Farinata), 42
  Soft Garlic Breadsticks, 58

Broccoli
  Green Curry with Tofu, 162
  Ma Po Tofu, 166
Bruschetta, 54

Brussels Sprouts

  Caramelized Brussels Sprouts
    with Cranberries, 92
  Curried Cauliflower and
    Brussels Sprouts, 78
  Roasted Vegetable Salad with
    Capers and Walnuts, 90
Buttermilk Pancakes, 24

Butternut Squash
  Balsamic Butternut Squash,
    94
  Jamaican Black Bean Stew,
    118
  Rainbow Vegetable Stew,
    130
  Roasted Squash with Tahini
    Couscous, 184

C

Cabbage
  Colorful Coleslaw, 98
  Crunchy Orange-Ginger Slaw,
    74
  Soba Stir-Fry, 160

Cake
  Apple Cake, 230
  Carrot Ginger Cupcakes, 226
  Chocolate Cake, 244
  Easy Orange Cake, 224
  Glazed Applesauce Spice
    Cake, 238
  Pineapple Upside Down Cake,
    219
Caramelized Brussels Sprouts
  with Cranberries, 92

Carrots
  Carrot Ginger Cupcakes, 226
  Crunchy Orange-Ginger Slaw,
    74
  Farro, Grape and Roasted
    Carrot Bowl, 208
  Lentil Soup, 128
  Pickled Carrots and
    Cucumbers, 199

Carrots *(continued)*
Red Beans and Rice with Pickled Carrots and Cucumbers, 198
Roasted Fennel and Spaghetti, 164
Sesame Ginger Tofu Báhn Mì, 144
Carrot Ginger Cupcakes, 226
Cauliflower
Cauliflower Tacos with Chipotle Crema, 146
Curried Cauliflower and Brussels Sprouts, 78
Fried Cauliflower Rice, 182
Cauliflower Tacos with Chipotle Crema, 146
Chai Brown Rice Pudding, 242
Chickpea Salad, 148
Chickpeas
Chickpea Salad, 148
Chickpea Tikka Masala, 210
Classic Hummus, 66
Pasta e Ceci, 122
Persimmon and Chickpea Salad, 110
Roasted Chickpea and Sweet Potato Bowl, 194
Spicy Roasted Chickpeas, 50
Chickpea Tikka Masala, 210
Chocolate
Chocolate-Almond Crispy Treats, 222
Chocolate Cake, 244
Chocolate Chip Cookies, 248
Coconut Milk Ice Cream, 220
Double Chocolate Cookies and Cream Mousse, 236
Chocolate-Almond Crispy Treats, 222
Chocolate Cake, 244
Chocolate Chip Cookies, 248
Chopped Salad with Cornbread Croutons, 106

Cilantro Peanut Pesto on Soba, 186
Classic Hummus, 66
Coconut
Chickpea Tikka Masala, 210
Chocolate Cake, 244
Coconut Milk Ice Cream, 220
Coconut, Peanut Butter and Quinoa Truffles, 232
Green Curry with Tofu, 162
Maple Pecan Granola, 26
Pumpkin Curry, 178
Coconut Milk Ice Cream, 220
Coconut, Peanut Butter and Quinoa Truffles, 232
Cold Peanut Noodles with Edamame, 172
Colorful Coleslaw, 98
Cookies
Chocolate Chip Cookies, 248
Triple Ginger Cookies, 234
Corn
Garden Vegetable Soup, 116
Quinoa and Roasted Corn, 102
Quinoa Burrito Bowls, 193
Rainbow Vegetable Stew, 130
Texas Caviar, 76
Tortilla Cups with Corn and Black Bean Salsa, 56
Cornbread, 107
Couscous
Roasted Squash with Tahini Couscous, 184
Toasted Peanut Couscous Salad, 80
Creamy Cashew Spread, 60
Creamy Tomato Soup, 134
Crispy Skillet Potatoes, 104
Crostini
Avocado Toast, 17
Beans and Greens Crostini, 44
Bruschetta, 54

Crunchy Orange-Ginger Slaw, 74
Cucumber Basil Cooler, 36
Cucumber Relish, 196
Cucumbers
Cucumber Basil Cooler, 36
Cucumber Relish, 196
Fattoush Salad, 73
Greek Salad with Tofu "Feta," 88
Mujadara, 202
Onion Fritters with Raita, 46
Pickled Carrots and Cucumbers, 199
Quinoa Tabbouleh, 108
Red Beans and Rice with Pickled Carrots and Cucumbers, 198
Sesame Ginger Tofu Báhn Mì, 144
Sesame Noodle Bowl, 214
Sharp Apple Cooler, 34
Szechuan Vegetable Noodles, 159
Tofu Satay Bowl, 196
Curly Curry Chips, 39
Curried Cauliflower and Brussels Sprouts, 78
Curry
Curried Cauliflower and Brussels Sprouts, 78
Green Curry with Tofu, 162
Pumpkin Curry, 178

D
Double Chocolate Cookies and Cream Mousse, 236
Double Green Pineapple Juice, 33
Dragon Tofu, 200
Dried Fruit
Barley with Currants and Pine Nuts, 86
Caramelized Brussels Sprouts with Cranberries, 92

Dried Fruit (continued)
Chopped Salad with Cornbread Croutons, 106
Crunchy Orange-Ginger Slaw, 74
Fruity Whole-Grain Cereal, 30
Jamaican Black Bean Stew, 118
Sweet and Savory Sweet Potato Salad, 82
Wheat Berry Apple Salad, 84

E
Easy Orange Cake, 224
Eggless Egg Salad Sandwich, 140
Eggplant: Roasted Vegetable Ramen Bowl, 206
Exotic Veggie Chips, 48

F
Farro
Farro Veggie Burgers, 139
Farro, Grape and Roasted Carrot Bowl, 208
Farro Veggie Burgers, 139
Farro, Grape and Roasted Carrot Bowl, 208
Fattoush Salad, 73
Fennel: Roasted Fennel and Spaghetti, 164
Four-Bean Chili, 126
French Toast Sticks, 28
Fried Cauliflower Rice, 182
Fried Tofu with Sesame Dipping Sauce, 40
Fruity Whole-Grain Cereal, 30

G
Garden Vegetable Soup, 116
Glazed Applesauce Spice Cake, 238
Gluten-Free Recipes
Balsamic Butternut Squash, 94
Caramelized Brussels Sprouts with Cranberries, 92
Chickpea Tikka Masala, 210

Gluten-Free Recipes (continued)
Chocolate-Almond Crispy Treats, 222
Cilantro Peanut Pesto on Soba, 186
Classic Hummus, 66
Colorful Coleslaw, 98
Creamy Cashew Spread, 60
Crispy Skillet Potatoes, 104
Curried Cauliflower and Brussels Sprouts, 78
Dragon Tofu, 200
Exotic Veggie Chips, 48
Fried Cauliflower Rice, 182
Greek Salad with Tofu "Feta," 88
Green Beans with Garlic-Cilantro Sauce, 96
Lentil Soup, 128
Maple Pecan Granola, 26
Mixed Berry Crisp, 228
Mujadara, 202
Onion Fritters with Raita, 46
Peanut Butter Tofu Bowl, 212
Persimmon and Chickpea Salad, 110
Picante Pintos and Rice, 204
Pickled Carrots and Cucumbers, 199
Quinoa and Roasted Corn, 102
Quinoa Burrito Bowls, 193
Quinoa Tabbouleh, 108
Rainbow Vegetable Stew, 130
Red Beans and Rice with Pickled Carrots and Cucumbers, 198
Roasted Chickpea and Sweet Potato Bowl, 194
Roasted Sweet Potato and Apple Salad, 100
Roasted Vegetable Salad with Capers and Walnuts, 90
Scrambled Tofu and Potatoes, 20
Socca (Farinata), 42

Gluten-Free Recipes (continued)
Spicy Roasted Chickpeas, 50
Super Oatmeal, 22
Sweet and Savory Sweet Potato Salad, 82
Texas Caviar, 76
Greek Salad with Tofu "Feta," 88
Green Beans
Garden Vegetable Soup, 116
Green Beans with Garlic-Cilantro Sauce, 96
Green Curry with Tofu, 162
Minestrone Soup, 124
Green Beans with Garlic-Cilantro Sauce, 96
Green Curry with Tofu, 162
Greens. See also **Kale; Spinach.**
Peanut Butter Tofu Bowl, 212
West African Peanut Soup, 132

J
Jamaican Black Bean Stew, 118
Jicama
Colorful Coleslaw, 98
Vegetable Rice Noodle Stir-Fry, 176
Juices
Cucumber Basil Cooler, 36
Double Green Pineapple Juice, 33
Melonade, 35
Morning Juice Blend, 37
Orchard Crush Juice, 32
Sharp Apple Cooler, 34
Tangerapple Juice, 33

K
Kale
Beans and Greens Crostini, 44
Double Green Pineapple Juice, 33
Picante Pintos and Rice, 204
Ribollita (Tuscan Bread Soup), 136
Koshari, 216

L

Lentil Bolognese, 190
Lentil Burgers, 150
Lentil Soup, 128
Lentils
  Koshari, 216
  Lentil Bolognese, 190
  Lentil Burgers, 150
  Lentil Soup, 128
  Mujadara, 202

M

Mac and Cheez, 180
Ma Po Tofu, 166
Maple Pecan Granola, 26
Melonade, 35
Minestrone Soup, 124
Mixed Berry Crisp, 228
Morning Juice Blend, 37
Mujadara, 202
Mushroom Gratin, 174
Mushroom Tofu Burgers, 142
Mushrooms
  Barbecue Seitan Skewers, 70
  Cauliflower Tacos with
    Chipotle Crema, 146
  Lentil Bolognese, 190
  Mushroom Gratin, 174
  Mushroom Tofu Burgers, 142
  Roasted Vegetable Ramen
    Bowl, 206
  Seitan Fajita Wraps, 156
  Soba Stir-Fry, 160
  Spinach Veggie Wrap, 152
  Tofu Satay Bowl, 196
  Vegetable and Nut Roast, 112

N

Nuts
  Apple Cake, 230
  Barley with Currants and Pine
    Nuts, 86
  Chocolate-Almond Crispy
    Treats, 222

Nuts *(continued)*
  Chopped Salad with
    Cornbread Croutons, 106
  Creamy Cashew Spread, 60
  Farro, Grape and Roasted
    Carrot Bowl, 208
  Glazed Applesauce Spice
    Cake, 238
  Maple Pecan Granola, 26
  Mixed Berry Crisp, 228
  Pecan Waffles, 18
  Pesto Fettuccine, 188
  Plum Rhubarb Crumble, 246
  Super Oatmeal, 22
  Vegetable and Nut Roast, 112

O

Oats
  Fruity Whole-Grain Cereal, 30
  Maple Pecan Granola, 26
  Mushroom Tofu Burgers, 142
  Plum Rhubarb Crumble, 246
  Super Oatmeal, 22
  Vegetable and Nut Roast, 112
Onion Fritters with Raita, 46
Orange
  Carrot Ginger Cupcakes, 226
  Crunchy Orange-Ginger Slaw,
    74
  Easy Orange Cake, 224
  Morning Juice Blend, 37
  Orange No-Butter Buttercream
    Frosting, 224
  Tangerapple Juice, 33
  Tofu Orange Dream, 36
Orange No-Butter Buttercream
  Frosting, 224
Orchard Crush Juice, 32

P

Pasta and Noodles
  Crunchy Orange-Ginger Slaw,
    74
  Koshari, 216

Pasta and Noodles *(continued)*
  Lentil Bolognese, 190
  Mac and Cheez, 180
  Minestrone Soup, 124
  Mushroom Gratin, 174
  Pasta e Ceci, 122
  Pesto Fettuccine, 188
  Roasted Fennel and Spaghetti,
    164
  Roasted Vegetable Ramen
    Bowl, 206
  Sesame Noodle Bowl, 214
  Spinach-Artichoke Lasagna,
    168
  Summer Spaghetti, 170
  Szechuan Cold Noodles, 159
  Szechuan Vegetable Noodles,
    159
Pasta e Ceci, 122
Peanut Butter Banana Blend, 37
Peanut Butter Tofu Bowl, 212
Peanuts and Peanut Butter
  Cilantro Peanut Pesto on Soba,
    186
  Coconut, Peanut Butter and
    Quinoa Truffles, 232
  Cold Peanut Noodles with
    Edamame, 172
  Peanut Butter Banana Blend,
    37
  Peanut Butter Tofu Bowl, 212
  Toasted Peanut Couscous
    Salad, 80
  Tofu Peanut Butter Smoothie,
    32
  Tofu Satay Bowl, 196
  West African Peanut Soup, 132
Peas
  Avocado Toast, 17
  Fried Cauliflower Rice, 182
  Pumpkin Curry, 178
Pecan Waffles, 18
Persimmon and Chickpea Salad,
  110
Pesto Fettuccine, 188

Picante Pintos and Rice, 204
Pickled Carrots and Cucumbers, 199

Pineapple
Double Green Pineapple Juice, 33
Morning Juice Blend, 37
Pineapple Upside Down Cake, 219
Tofu, Fruit and Veggie Smoothie, 35

Pineapple Upside Down Cake, 219
Pita Bread, 64
Plum Rhubarb Crumble, 246

Potatoes
Crispy Skillet Potatoes, 104
Curly Curry Chips, 39
Farro Veggie Burgers, 139
Roasted Vegetable Salad with Capers and Walnuts, 90
Scrambled Tofu and Potatoes, 20

Pumpkin Curry, 178

Q
Quinoa
Coconut, Peanut Butter and Quinoa Truffles, 232
Quinoa and Roasted Corn, 102
Quinoa Burrito Bowls, 193
Quinoa Patties with Roasted Red Pepper Sauce, 68
Quinoa Tabbouleh, 108
Rainbow Vegetable Stew, 130
Roasted Chickpea and Sweet Potato Bowl, 194

Quinoa and Roasted Corn, 102
Quinoa Burrito Bowls, 193
Quinoa Patties with Roasted Red Pepper Sauce, 68
Quinoa Tabbouleh, 108

R
Rainbow Vegetable Stew, 130
Red Beans and Rice with Pickled Carrots and Cucumbers, 198
Ribollita (Tuscan Bread Soup), 136

Rice
Chai Brown Rice Pudding, 242
Dragon Tofu, 200
Fruity Whole-Grain Cereal, 30
Green Curry with Tofu, 162
Jamaican Black Bean Stew, 118
Koshari, 216
Mujadara, 202
Peanut Butter Tofu Bowl, 212
Picante Pintos and Rice, 204
Red Beans and Rice with Pickled Carrots and Cucumbers, 198

Rice Noodles
Cold Peanut Noodles with Edamame, 172
Vegetable Rice Noodle Stir-Fry, 176

Roasted Chickpea and Sweet Potato Bowl, 194
Roasted Fennel and Spaghetti, 164
Roasted Squash with Tahini Couscous, 184
Roasted Sweet Potato and Apple Salad, 100
Roasted Vegetable Ramen Bowl, 206
Roasted Vegetable Salad with Capers and Walnuts, 90

S
Scallion Pancakes, 62
Scrambled Tofu and Potatoes, 20

Seitan
Barbecue Seitan Skewers, 70
Seitan Fajita Wraps, 156

Seitan Fajita Wraps, 156
Sesame Ginger Tofu Bánh Mì, 144
Sesame Noodle Bowl, 214
Sharp Apple Cooler, 34
Sloppy Joes, 154

Smoothies
Berry Soy-Cream Blend, 34
Peanut Butter Banana Blend, 37
Tofu Orange Dream, 36
Tofu Peanut Butter Smoothie, 32
Tofu, Fruit and Veggie Smoothie, 35

Soba Noodles
Cilantro Peanut Pesto on Soba, 186
Soba Stir-Fry, 160

Soba Stir-Fry, 160
Socca (Farinata), 42
Soft Garlic Breadsticks, 58
Spicy Roasted Chickpeas, 50

Spinach
Dragon Tofu, 200
Minestrone Soup, 124
Spinach Veggie Wrap, 152
Spinach-Artichoke Lasagna, 168

Spinach Veggie Wrap, 152
Spinach-Artichoke Lasagna, 168
Summer Spaghetti, 170
Super Oatmeal, 22
Sweet and Savory Sweet Potato Salad, 82

Sweet Potatoes
Chopped Salad with Cornbread Croutons, 106
Exotic Veggie Chips, 48
Jamaican Black Bean Stew, 118

Sweet Potatoes *(continued)*
Roasted Chickpea and Sweet Potato Bowl, 194
Roasted Sweet Potato and Apple Salad, 100
Sweet and Savory Sweet Potato Salad, 82
Vegetable Rice Noodle Stir-Fry, 176
West African Peanut Soup, 132
Szechuan Cold Noodles, 159
Szechuan Vegetable Noodles, 159

T
Tahini
Classic Hummus, 66
Persimmon and Chickpea Salad, 110
Roasted Chickpea and Sweet Potato Bowl, 194
Roasted Squash with Tahini Couscous, 184
Tangerapple Juice, 33
Texas Caviar, 76
Toasted Peanut Couscous Salad, 80
Tofu
Berry Soy-Cream Blend, 34
Chickpea Tikka Masala, 210
Dragon Tofu, 200
Eggless Egg Salad Sandwich, 140
Fried Cauliflower Rice, 182
Fried Tofu with Sesame Dipping Sauce, 40
Greek Salad with Tofu "Feta," 88
Green Curry with Tofu, 162
Ma Po Tofu, 166
Mushroom Tofu Burgers, 142
Not-Ricotta, 168
Peanut Butter Tofu Bowl, 212
Pumpkin Curry, 178

Tofu *(continued)*
Scrambled Tofu and Potatoes, 20
Sesame Ginger Tofu Bánh Mì, 144
Sesame Noodle Bowl, 214
Soba Stir-Fry, 160
Spinach-Artichoke Lasagna, 168
Tofu, Fruit and Veggie Smoothie, 35
Tofu Orange Dream, 36
Tofu Peanut Butter Smoothie, 32
Tofu Satay Bowl, 196
Vegetable Rice Noodle Stir-Fry, 176
Tofu, Fruit and Veggie Smoothie, 35
Tofu Orange Dream, 36
Tofu Peanut Butter Smoothie, 32
Tofu Satay Bowl, 196
Tomatoes
Bruschetta, 54
Chickpea Tikka Masala, 210
Chopped Salad with Cornbread Croutons, 106
Creamy Tomato Soup, 134
Fattoush Salad, 73
Four-Bean Chili, 126
Garden Vegetable Soup, 116
Greek Salad with Tofu "Feta,"88
Koshari, 216
Lentil Bolognese, 190
Minestrone Soup, 124
Pasta e Ceci, 122
Picante Pintos and Rice, 204
Quinoa and Roasted Corn, 102
Quinoa Tabbouleh, 108
Ribollita (Tuscan Bread Soup), 136

Tomatoes *(continued)*
Spinach Veggie Wrap, 152
Spinach-Artichoke Lasagna, 168
Summer Spaghetti, 170
Texas Caviar, 76
Vegetable and Nut Roast, 112
West African Peanut Soup, 132
White Beans and Tomatoes, 120
Tortilla Cups with Corn and Black Bean Salsa, 56
Tortillas
Cauliflower Tacos with Chipotle Crema, 146
Seitan Fajita Wraps, 156
Spinach Veggie Wrap, 152
Tortilla Cups with Corn and Black Bean Salsa, 56
Triple Ginger Cookies, 234

V
Vegetable and Nut Roast, 112
Vegetable Rice Noodle Stir-Fry, 176

W
West African Peanut Soup, 132
Wheat Berry Apple Salad, 84
White Beans and Tomatoes, 120

Z
Zucchini
Barbecue Seitan Skewers, 70
Dragon Tofu, 200
Garden Vegetable Soup, 116
Minestrone Soup, 124
Ribollita (Tuscan Bread Soup), 136
Roasted Vegetable Ramen Bowl, 206

METRIC CONVERSION CHART

VOLUME MEASUREMENTS (dry)

$\frac{1}{8}$ teaspoon = 0.5 mL
$\frac{1}{4}$ teaspoon = 1 mL
$\frac{1}{2}$ teaspoon = 2 mL
$\frac{3}{4}$ teaspoon = 4 mL
1 teaspoon = 5 mL
1 tablespoon = 15 mL
2 tablespoons = 30 mL
$\frac{1}{4}$ cup = 60 mL
$\frac{1}{3}$ cup = 75 mL
$\frac{1}{2}$ cup = 125 mL
$\frac{2}{3}$ cup = 150 mL
$\frac{3}{4}$ cup = 175 mL
1 cup = 250 mL
2 cups = 1 pint = 500 mL
3 cups = 750 mL
4 cups = 1 quart = 1 L

VOLUME MEASUREMENTS (fluid)

1 fluid ounce (2 tablespoons) = 30 mL
4 fluid ounces ($\frac{1}{2}$ cup) = 125 mL
8 fluid ounces (1 cup) = 250 mL
12 fluid ounces ($1\frac{1}{2}$ cups) = 375 mL
16 fluid ounces (2 cups) = 500 mL

WEIGHTS (mass)

$\frac{1}{2}$ ounce = 15 g
1 ounce = 30 g
3 ounces = 90 g
4 ounces = 120 g
8 ounces = 225 g
10 ounces = 285 g
12 ounces = 360 g
16 ounces = 1 pound = 450 g

DIMENSIONS

$\frac{1}{16}$ inch = 2 mm
$\frac{1}{8}$ inch = 3 mm
$\frac{1}{4}$ inch = 6 mm
$\frac{1}{2}$ inch = 1.5 cm
$\frac{3}{4}$ inch = 2 cm
1 inch = 2.5 cm

OVEN TEMPERATURES

250°F = 120°C
275°F = 140°C
300°F = 150°C
325°F = 160°C
350°F = 180°C
375°F = 190°C
400°F = 200°C
425°F = 220°C
450°F = 230°C

BAKING PAN SIZES

Utensil	Size in Inches/Quarts	Metric Volume	Size in Centimeters
Baking or Cake Pan (square or rectangular)	8×8×2	2 L	20×20×5
	9×9×2	2.5 L	23×23×5
	12×8×2	3 L	30×20×5
	13×9×2	3.5 L	33×23×5
Loaf Pan	8×4×3	1.5 L	20×10×7
	9×5×3	2 L	23×13×7
Round Layer Cake Pan	8×1½	1.2 L	20×4
	9×1½	1.5 L	23×4
Pie Plate	8×1¼	750 mL	20×3
	9×1¼	1 L	23×3
Baking Dish or Casserole	1 quart	1 L	—
	1½ quart	1.5 L	—
	2 quart	2 L	—